THE
LIFE BEYOND

ROBERT L. MILLET & JOSEPH FIELDING McCONKIE

THE LIFE BEYOND

ROBERT L. MILLET & JOSEPH FIELDING McCONKIE

DESERET
BOOK

SALT LAKE CITY, UTAH

Cover photo by Eldon Linschoten

Graphics by Allan Loyborg

First printing in hardbound 1986
First printing in paperbound 2005

Visit us at DeseretBook.com

Library of Congress Catalog Card Number: 86-71161

ISBN 0-88494-601-0 (hardbound)
ISBN 978-1-59038-256-1 (paperbound)

Printed in the United States of America
LSC Communications, Crawfordsville, IN

44 43

This book is affectionately dedicated to
Elder Bruce R. McConkie (1915–1985), from whom we
inherited a love for these principles and the
desire to teach and testify of them

Death hath passed upon all men, to fulfil the merciful plan of the great Creator.

—Jacob (2 Nephi 9:6)

May I say for the consolation of those who mourn, and for the comfort and guidance of all of us, that no righteous man is ever taken before his time. In the case of the faithful saints, they are simply transferred to other fields of labor. The Lord's work goes on in this life, in the world of spirits, and in the kingdoms of glory where men go after their resurrection.

—Joseph Fielding Smith
(in his remarks at the funeral
services for Elder Richard L. Evans)

Contents

Preface

From time immemorial no subject has captivated the interest and attention of men like that of the life beyond. Kings and princes, philosophers and scholars, theologians and Saints, laymen and peasants—all have sought, with Job, to know, "If a man die, shall he live again?" (Job 14:14). And if there is a future state, what is its nature? And how best may mortal man prepare for it? Indeed, death has ever remained life's most awesome mystery. In the absence of revelation, man's would-be gaze into future worlds is unable to penetrate the darkness of the grave.

The spring of 1820 heralded the dawning of a brighter day, as celestial light pierced the blackness of the long night of heaven's silence. In the midst of that light stood two eternal beings whose very presence attested to the reality of the life beyond, as would the subsequent appearances of various messengers who would be sent to bestow the knowledge, keys, and powers pertaining to the eternal worlds. With the restoration of these heaven-sent truths, the shadows of doubt and skepticism have fled, and once again the warmth of heaven's light, with its glad tidings of great joy, is felt by men of peace and good will. Thus the living and the dead break forth in anthems of eternal praise to their King Immanuel. The mysteries of God have begun to be unfolded, and the Saints of the Most High are made partakers of that knowledge which eye hath not seen, nor ear heard, neither hath entered into the heart of unillumined man.

Let there be no mistake. Because of the opening of the heavens—the Vision of the Glories, the Vision of the Celestial Kingdom, the Prophet's discourse at the funeral of King Follett, the Vision of the Redemption of the Dead, our latter-day prophets and current prophecy—those of the household of faith have their perceptions and understanding extended beyond the bounds of the Bible and of the visions of earth's most noble and inspired writers and religious leaders. We rejoice in the teachings and testimonies of all who have been commissioned to bear witness of heavenly things, but we owe a special debt of gratitude to the Prophet Joseph Smith and President Joseph F. Smith for their unique contributions to our understanding of these precious verities.

In that which we have written, we have sought to say "none other things than that which the prophets and apostles have written, and that which is taught" us "by the Comforter through the prayer of faith" (D&C 52:9). We alone assume responsibility for what follows, believing the principles contained herein to be true according to the best of our knowledge.

1

Parting the Veil

The power and authority of the higher, or Melchizedek Priesthood, is to hold the keys of all the spiritual blessings of the church—to have the privilege of receiving the mysteries of the kingdom of heaven, to have the heavens opened unto them.

—D&C 107:18–19

Thanks be to God—the heavens have been opened! With the restoration of light and truth and sacred priesthood powers have come the keys which enable man to glimpse into past and future and which provide a divine perspective for the present. Through prophets and priesthood the Lord's people have been invited again to both comprehend and stand in the presence of their God. "This greater priesthood," the revelations state, "administereth the gospel and holdeth the key of the mysteries of the kingdom, even the key of the knowledge of God" (D&C 84:19). In another revelation on priesthood given to Joseph Smith, the Lord explained: "The power and authority of the higher, or Melchizedek Priesthood, is to hold the keys of all the spiritual blessings of the church—to have the privilege of receiving the mysteries of the kingdom of heaven" (D&C 107:18–19).

Our Invitation to the Divine Presence

Enoch was caught away to a high mountain and shown things from his time to the end (Moses 7). Moses was likewise "caught up into an exceedingly high mountain" and saw the Lord Jehovah and the works of his divine hands (Moses 1). Peter, James, and John beheld marvelous things on the holy mount, including the eventual transfiguration of the earth and its inhabitants (Matthew 17:1–9; 2 Peter 1:16–19; D&C 63:20–21). The message of the Restoration is that God has opened the heavens again and has called holy men to stand with him on the high mountain, that he might make known his mind and will and purposes. As the ancient prophets and Apostles were permitted a view of eternity, so also in our day have modern oracles penetrated the veil, been witnesses of the world beyond this sphere, and beckoned us to come and be partakers also of that knowledge which both saves and satisfies the soul.

All men know they must die. It is but appropriate that God should reveal something on the subject. And so he has. That which he has revealed constitutes a perfect witness of the restoration of the everlasting gospel and the attendant truths which manifest to man his eternal nature and glorious potential beyond the veil of death. Again the heavens have been opened, the veil parted, and men and women of faith invited to look beyond and know of that which awaits them hereafter. As Lehi in dream partook of that fruit which was sweet above all other, so we too may feast upon that which is most joyous to the soul. Through those precious truths contained in such revelations as the Vision of the Glories (D&C 76), the Vision of the Celestial Kingdom (D&C 137), the King Follett Sermon, and the Vision of the Redemption of the Dead (D&C 138)—each plucked from the tree of life —we are invited to feast upon that same fruit.

The Vision of the Glories

Less than two years passed from the time of the formal organization of the restored Church until the God of glory chose to open the heavens and expand the spiritual horizons of the Saints in a transcendent manner. It was the winter of 1832. Joseph Smith had been engaged in his work of inspired translation of the Bible since June of 1830, and since April of 1831 had concentrated on the New Testament. Joseph and Emma were then living in the home of John Johnson in Hiram, Ohio. On February 16 in the year 1832 Joseph the Prophet and Sidney Rigdon his scribe prayerfully pondered the fifth chapter of John's Gospel, particularly verse 29. By the power of the Spirit the translators felt impressed to alter the King James verse so as to refer to the "resurrection of the *just*" and the "resurrection of the *unjust,*" instead of the resurrections of life and damnation. This change "caused us to marvel," the Prophet said, "for it was given unto us of the Spirit. And while we meditated upon these things, the Lord touched the eyes of our understandings and they were opened, and the glory of the Lord shone round about." (D&C 76:18–19.)

Philo Dibble has given the following description of the occasion:

> The vision which is recorded in the book of Doctrine and Covenants was given at the house of "Father Johnson," in Hyrum [sic], Ohio, and during the time that Joseph and Sidney were in the spirit and saw the heavens open, there were other men in the room, perhaps twelve, among whom I was one during a part of the time—probably two-thirds of the time—I saw the glory and felt the power, but did not see the vision.
>
> The events and conversation, while they were seeing what is written (and many things were seen and related that are not written), I will relate as minutely as is necessary.
>
> Joseph would, at intervals, say: "What do I see?" as one might say while looking out the window and beholding what all in the room could not see. Then he would relate what he had seen or what he was looking at. Then Sidney replied, "I see the same." Presently Sidney would say: "What do I see?" and would repeat what he had seen or was seeing, and Joseph would reply, "I see the same."
>
> This manner of conversation was repeated at short intervals to the end of the vision, and during the whole time not a

word was spoken by any other person. Not a sound nor motion was made by anyone but Joseph and Sidney, and it seemed to me that they never moved a joint or limb during the time I was there, which I think was over an hour, and to the end of the vision.[1]

That which burst upon the minds and hearts of Joseph Smith and Sidney Rigdon also burst the shackles of ignorance and fear and provided specific doctrinal instruction concerning the "Great Plan of the Eternal God." The Vision of the Glories consists of a series of manifestations: (1) a glorious vision of the throne of God, Christ at his right hand, and holy angels praising and worshiping their God; (2) a dramatically contrasting scene—the fall of Lucifer and the sons of perdition, those who chose to deny and defy the Lord and his plan, and who with malevolent mentality seek to crucify the Christ anew; (3) then, as the glory of the day follows the darkness of night, a vision of the celestial world, as well as an understanding of those who qualify for such wonders and blessings; (4) a vision of the terrestrial world with its honorable hosts; (5) a vision of the telestial world and its inhabitants, those who lived in dishonor and were untouched by spiritual truths; and (6) an understanding of hell—its composition and duration. The Vision of the Glories takes us from premortality to residence in the eternal worlds and thus provides through its breadth and depth the answers to a multitude of questions. "Nothing could be more pleasing to the Saints upon the order of the kingdom of the Lord," Joseph Smith exulted, "than the light which burst upon the world through the foregoing vision."

> Every law, every commandment, every promise, every truth, and every point touching the destiny of man, from Genesis to Revelation, where the purity of the scriptures remains unsullied by the folly of men, go to show the perfection of the theory [of different degrees of glory in the resurrection] and witnesses the fact that *that document is a transcript from the records of the eternal world*. The sublimity of the ideas; the purity of the language; the scope for action; the continued duration for completion, in order that the heirs of salvation

may confess the Lord and bow the knee; the rewards for faithfulness, and the punishments for sins, are so much beyond the
narrow-mindedness of men that every honest man is con-
strained to exclaim: "It came from God."[2]

The Vision of the Celestial Kingdom

The headquarters of the Church moved from New York
and Pennsylvania to Ohio. By 1831 two Church centers were
organized, one in Kirtland and the other in Missouri (Zion).
A commandment came as early as 1833 to build a temple.
The Lord instructed that they "should build a house, in the
which house I design to endow those whom I have chosen
with power from on high" (D&C 95:8). The sacrifice of the
Saints to erect the holy edifice was not ignored by that Lord
who knows all, and the blessings of heaven were poured out
upon the Latter-day Saints in the form of a remarkable period
of pentecost. In summarizing this period, Milton V. Backman
has written:

> During a fifteen-week period, extending from January 21
> to May 1, 1836, probably more Latter-day Saints beheld visions
> and witnessed other unusual spiritual manifestations than
> during any other era in the history of the Church. There were
> reports of Saints' beholding heavenly beings at ten different
> meetings held during that time. At eight of these meetings,
> many reported seeing angels; at five of the services, individu-
> als testified that Jesus, the Savior, appeared. While the Saints
> were thus communing with heavenly hosts, many prophesied,
> some spoke in tongues, and others received the gift of inter-
> pretation of tongues.[3]

Joseph and his brethren commenced meeting in the
temple even before its completion, where they participated
in washings, anointings, and blessings. On Thursday, 21
January 1836, the Prophet and a number of Church leaders
had gathered in the third (attic) floor of the Kirtland Temple.
Joseph Smith explained concerning this occasion:

> At early candle-light I met with the Presidency at the west
> school room, in the Temple, to attend to the ordinance of
> anointing our heads with holy oil; also the [High] Councils of

Kirtland and Zion met in the two adjoining rooms, and waited in prayer while we attended to the ordinance. I took the oil in my left hand, Father Smith being seated before me, and the remainder of the Presidency encircled him round about. We then stretched our right hands towards heaven, and blessed the oil, and consecrated it in the name of Jesus Christ.

We then laid our hands upon our aged Father Smith, and invoked the blessings of heaven. I then anointed his head with the consecrated oil, and sealed many blessings upon him. The Presidency then in turn laid their hands upon his head, . . . and pronounced such blessings upon his head, as the Lord put into their hearts, all blessing him to be our Patriarch, to anoint our heads, and attend to all duties that pertain to that office. The Presidency then . . . received their anointing and blessing under the hands of Father Smith. And in turn, my father anointed my head, and sealed upon me the blessings of Moses, to lead Israel in the latter days, even as Moses led him in days of old; also the blessings of Abraham, Isaac, and Jacob. All of the Presidency laid their hands upon me, and pronounced upon my head many prophecies and blessings, many of which I shall not notice at this time. But as Paul said, so say I, let us come to visions and revelations.[4]

Joseph then said: "The heavens were opened upon us, and I beheld the celestial kingdom of God, and the glory thereof" (D&C 137:1).

The doctrinal restoration which commenced in the spring of 1820 (and will accelerate even through the Millennium[5]) continued. In this vision, Joseph the Seer—having been anointed, the symbolic representation of the outpouring of the Spirit—again became witness of the majesty of the celestial world. He saw the throne of God and envisioned that which would yet be, as prophetic personalities and members of his own family stood in the divine presence. The Vision of the Celestial Kingdom is, in addition, a confirming witness of the law of justification. Just as no person will achieve exaltation without a willing and obedient heart, even so no person will be denied a blessing or opportunity because of circumstances beyond his or her control; no person in all eternity will be held accountable for a law or will be denied privileges of which he or she was ignorant. We glory in the reality that God judges men according to the desires of the heart, as well as the works done in the flesh.

The King Follett Sermon

On 9 March 1844 King Follett, a faithful member of the Church, was killed while digging a well in Nauvoo. Joseph the Prophet was obviously deeply touched by the death of Brother Follett. His passing evoked from Joseph the greatest discourse of his prophetic ministry. At the general conference of the Church (7 April 1844) the Prophet honored King Follett, and in the process delivered a masterful discourse, a sermon plain but profound in its implications. The setting for the conference has been described as follows:

> In the weeks immediately preceding April conference, a conspiracy developed against the Prophet. Those involved in the intrigue claimed that Joseph Smith was a fallen prophet, citing as evidence the practice of polygamy, the monopolistic economic policies of the Church, and the increase in his personal power. Hoping to raise popular support for their cause, the conspirators desired to confront the prophet during the conference.
>
> Good weather was a blessing for the Saints because their meetings were held outdoors. In fact, the Mormons did not build any meetinghouses in Nauvoo. Virtually all of the public meetings were held outdoors in areas referred to as "the groves." The Saints held meetings in three different groves located on the edges of the bluff to the northeast, west, and south of the temple. The sloping contours of the bluffs provided a natural amphitheater, to which the Saints added wooden benches and a speaker's rostrum.[6]

The Prophet rose that Sunday morning and spoke for over two hours to a crowd of from ten to twenty thousand people. One citizen of the "city of Joseph" who was present on this occasion has left her recollections:

> I was very small when we lived in Nauvoo, but I always attended the meetings. The most striking thing I remember

was a prophecy Joseph Smith made, which I saw fulfilled immediately. I was at the funeral service of King Follett, in the Nauvoo Grove. A heavy thunderstorm arose. The people became frightened and started to go home. But the Prophet arose and told the multitude that if they would remain still and pray in their hearts the storm would not molest them in their services.

They did as they were bidden, and the storm divided over the grove. I well remember how it was storming on all sides of the grove, yet it was calm around us as if there was no sign of a storm so near by.

I thought as I sat there that the Lord was speaking through Joseph.[7]

Those who came to the grove with dark motives and doubtful hearts found sufficient ammunition to perpetuate their claims of "fallen prophet." Those, on the other hand, who were loyal to their leader and entered the grove with eyes and ears of faith were richly rewarded. They witnessed their beloved Prophet at the zenith of his ministry, eloquent in his presentation of deep and penetrating doctrine, and bold in defense of his own prophetic calling. It was on this occasion that the veil was parted for the Saints once again, and the Prophet Joseph beckoned to the members to see what he had come to know by revelation. Brother Joseph opened the scriptures to the understanding of many and expounded upon several doctrinal points during the time he occupied the stand, including the nature of eternal life, dwelling in everlasting burnings, the manner in which the Gods planned and created the earth, the eternal nature of man and element, and the unpardonable sin. Most important, however, Joseph Smith lifted his hearers to a loftier level of comprehension concerning Deity: he explained how God came to be God, the mystery associated with the fact that "God himself was once as we are now, and is an exalted man, and sits enthroned in yonder heavens."[8] In addition, the Prophet taught those assembled that through righteousness man is exalted, coming to know and be like God himself.

The Vision of the Redemption of the Dead

During the last six months of his life, President Joseph F. Smith, nephew of the Prophet Joseph Smith and sixth President of the Church, suffered from the effects of advancing years (he was in his eightieth year). He spent much of his time in his personal study in the Beehive House. President Smith did manage to attend the October 1918 general conference. On Friday, 4 October, President Smith opened the conference with these words:

> As most of you, I suppose, are aware, I have been undergoing a siege of very serious illness for the past five months. It would be impossible for me, on this occasion, to occupy sufficient time to express the desires of my heart and my feelings, as I would desire to express them to you. . . .
>
> I will not, I dare not, attempt to enter upon many things that are resting upon my mind this morning, and I shall postpone until some future time, the Lord being willing, my attempt to tell you some of the things that are in my mind, and that dwell in my heart. *I have not lived alone these last five months. I have dwelt in the spirit of prayer, of supplication, of faith and of determination; and I have had my communication with the Spirit of the Lord continuously.*[2]

Joseph Fielding Smith indicated that his father was here expressing the fact that during the preceding half year he had been the recipient of numerous manifestations. One of these—the Vision of the Redemption of the Dead—had been received just the day before.

Joseph F. Smith's attention was drawn to the world beyond mortality by his frequent confrontation with death. His parents, Hyrum and Mary Fielding Smith, had both died by the time Joseph F. was a young man. His soul wrenched as he delivered a number of his own small children to the grave. Joseph Fielding Smith has written: "When death invaded his home, as frequently it did, and his little ones were taken from him, he grieved with a broken heart and mourned, not as those who mourn who live without hope, but for the loss of his 'precious jewels' dearer to him than life itself."[10] On 20 January 1918 Hyrum Mack Smith, oldest son of Joseph F. and then a member of the Council of the Twelve, was taken to the hospital for a serious illness, where the physician diagnosed a ruptured appendix. Despite constant medical attention and repeated pleadings in prayer, Hyrum M.—then only forty-five years old—died on the night of 23 January. This was a particularly traumatic trial for President Smith, "one of the most severe blows that he was ever called upon to endure."[11]

Standing in the twilight of life, men of nobility have been able to view existence with divine perspective, and thereby the finite mind has been opened to the things of infinity. "If we live our holy religion," Brigham Young taught, "and let the Spirit reign," the mind of man "will not become dull and stupid, but *as the body approaches dissolution the spirit takes a firmer hold on that enduring substance behind the vail,* drawing from the depths of that eternal Fountain of Light sparkling gems of intelligence which surround the frail and sinking tabernacle with a halo of immortal wisdom."[12] This poignant principle was beautifully demonstrated in the life of Joseph F. Smith. Truly, suffering sanctifies godly men. Here was a man who met death and sorrow and persecution with quiet dignity and thus through the fellowhip of Christ's suffering was made acquainted with the things of God.

On Thursday, 3 October 1918, President Smith, largely confined to his room because of illness, sat meditating over the universal nature of the Atonement, and the Apostle Peter's allusions to Christ's postmortal ministry in the world of spirits. Thus a lifelong preparation responded to the readiness of the moment, giving birth to a heavenly endowment—the Vision of the Redemption of the Dead. Understanding was added to understanding, faith to faith: additional knowledge came forth and already available truths were confirmed, clarified, and expanded. Our grasp and perspective on such matters as the nature and composition of the spirit world, as well as the administrative and instructional ministry of the Savior to that realm in the meridian of time, were broadened and strengthened.

Conclusion

The Lord warned the early Saints that their minds in times past had been darkened because of unbelief and because they had treated lightly the things they had received, namely, the Book of Mormon and the revelations of the Restoration. We live in a day when the glorious gospel light shines with a brilliance unknown in past ages, a time when "the dawning of a brighter day majestic rises on the world" *(Hymns,* 1985, no. 1). Unless we pay careful heed to "those things which are communicated" to us in this day and time, we proceed through life with less than optimal illumination: we find ourselves "walking in darkness at noon-day." (D&C 84:54–61; 95:6.) Our knowledge of things beyond the veil comes from latter-day revelation and living prophets. Through the revelations given to Joseph Smith and Joseph F. Smith—the particulars of which we will consider more completely hereafter as we construct the house of our understanding—we too may be able to see with prophetic eyes and have seerlike vision of the purposes and possibilities of that world beyond the grave.

2

The World of Spirits

Now, concerning the state of the soul between death and the resurrection—Behold, it has been made known unto me by an angel, that . . . the spirits of those who are righteous are received into a state of happiness, which is called paradise. . . . And then shall it come to pass, that the spirits of the wicked . . . shall be cast out into outer darkness; there shall be weeping, and wailing, and gnashing of teeth. . . . Thus they remain in this state, as well as the righteous in paradise, until the time of their resurrection.

—Alma 40:11–14

Might we ask with Alma: What becomes of man—the eternal spirit—at the time of death? Does it remain forever in a grave of darkness? Or does it continue to exist, and if so, does it retain its individuality? Does the spirit return immediately to the divine presence? And what of the world of spirits— where is it and what of its nature? Do all spirits—the good and the evil—comingle together, or have their works and desires led to a separation at death? And what of such a state—is it endless or will the spirit again reclaim its body? All such questions and many more are answered with clarity by the revelations of the Restoration, from which we learn of this afterworld, this life beyond the grave.

Life and Death

Birth and death are inextricably intertwined, the words being defined in terms of one another. First, we are born to die and die to live. Mortal birth is tantamount to a death in regard to premortality: we die as to things as they were in order to enter the realm of mortality. In so doing, we move from "eternity" into "time." Second, having been cut off from the presence of the Father through birth in our journey from the divine presence to this fallen world and thus having died as pertaining to the things of righteousness, we are in need of a new birth. To use Paul's language, we must crucify the old man of sin and come forth in a newness of life (see Romans 6:6) in order to go where God and angels dwell. Finally, we must pass beyond this veil of tears to inherit a far greater and grander existence; it is in dying that we are born unto eternal life. In mortal death we leave the realms of "time" and return to those of "eternity."

Life's starkest reality is death. Death is "a subject which strikes dread—even terror—into the hearts of most men. It is something we fear, of which we are sorely afraid, and from which most of us would flee if we could."[1] It is a universal commonality, one thing which every mortal shares with every other mortal, this in spite of earthly status and accomplishments. Every man or woman is born and every man and woman must die. All are born as helpless infants, and all are equally helpless in the face of death. Even among those who see by the lamp of gospel understanding, death is frequently viewed with fear and trembling. Joseph Smith is reported to have taught that "*the Lord in his wisdom had implanted the fear of death in every person that they might cling to life and thus accomplish the designs of their Creator.*"[2] The severance of fraternal and familial ties is of all things most painful for those who remain, bringing with it an avalanche of loneliness and sorrow. Such are the feelings even of men and women of faith. He who has the panoramic vision and the broadest perspective on life and death is aware of such agonies. The God of us all has said: "Thou shalt live together in love, insomuch that thou shalt weep for the loss of them that die" (D&C 42:45).

Life's bitter winters may find us walking alone. During these cold and dark seasons of solitude, we wrap ourselves in the protective clothing of faith and its perspective and are warmed by precious memories. Thus we move on, seeking always to view things as God views them. "Precious in the sight of the Lord," the revealed word declares, "is the death of his saints" (Psalm 116:15). "Blessed are the dead which die in the Lord," for they shall "rest from their labours; and their works do follow them" (Revelation 14:13).

Entrance into the World of Spirits

The transition from time into eternity is immediate. As the physical self breathes its last breath, the spirit self passes through a thin veil separating this world from the next. In the words of Parley P. Pratt: "The outward tabernacle, inhabited by a spirit, returns to the element from which it emanated. But the thinking being, the individual, active agent or identity that inhabited that tabernacle, never ceased to exist, to think, act, live, move, or have a being; never ceased to exercise those sympathies, affections, hopes, and aspirations, which are founded in the very nature of intelligences, being the inherent and invaluable principles of their eternal existence."[3] The powers of intellect and the feelings of the heart reside within the spirit of man, or what is most frequently called the *soul.* (See 1 Nephi 15:35; Mosiah 14:10; Alma 36:15; 40:7, 11–14, 18, 21, 23; 42:16; D&C 101:37; Abraham 3:23.)

Location of the Spirit World

And where is it that the spirit of man goes at death? Where is the world of spirits? Joseph Smith taught: "The spirits of the just are exalted to a greater and more glorious work; hence they are blessed in their departure to the world of spirits." The Prophet then added that *"they are not far from us,* and know and understand our thoughts, feelings, and motions, and are often pained therewith."⁴ In speaking of the nearness of the world of spirits, Parley P. Pratt wrote that *"it is here on the very planet where we were born."* Continuing, he explained: "The earth and all other planets of a like sphere, have their inward or spiritual spheres, as well as their outward, or temporal. The one is peopled by temporal tabernacles, and the other by spirits. A veil is drawn between the one sphere and the other, whereby all the objects in the spiritual sphere are rendered invisible to those in the temporal."⁵

Returning to the Presence of God?

The prophet Alma, recognizing that resurrection—the inseparable union of body and spirit—did not immediately follow death, inquired of the Lord concerning the "state of the soul between death and the resurrection." An angel, a citizen himself of the world of spirits, explained to Alma the nature of the afterworld. Thus Alma testified: "It has been made known unto me by an angel, that the spirits of all men, as soon as they are departed from this mortal body, yea, the spirits of all men, whether they be good or evil, are taken home to that God who gave them life" (Alma 40:11). Alma's language is similar to that of the Preacher in the book of Ecclesiastes: "Then shall the dust return to the earth as it was: and the spirit shall return unto God who gave it" (Ecclesiastes 2:7).

Both of these scriptural preachers are speaking in broadest terms, and should not be interpreted to mean that the spirit—at the time of death—goes into the immediate presence of the Lord. President Brigham Young explained that to speak of the spirit returning to the God who gave it means that "when the spirits leave their bodies they are in the presence of our Father and God" in the sense that they "are prepared then to see, hear and understand spiritual things."⁶ To go into the "presence" of God is not necessarily to be "placed within a few yards or rods, or within a short distance of his person."⁷ President George Q. Cannon explained: "Alma, when he says that 'the spirits of all men, as soon as they are departed from this mortal body, . . . are taken home to that God who gave them life,' has the idea, doubtless, in his mind that our God is omnipresent—not in His own personality but through His minister, the Holy Spirit. He does not intend to convey the idea that they are immediately ushered into the personal presence of God. He evidently uses that phrase in a qualified sense."[8] Similarly, Heber C. Kimball taught: "As for my going into the immediate presence of God when I die, I do not expect it, but I expect to go into the world of spirits and associate with my brethren, and preach the Gospel in the spiritual world, and prepare myself in every necessary way to receive my body again, and then enter through the wall into the celestial world. I never shall come into the presence of my Father and God until I have received my resurrected body, neither will any other person."[9]

One World

The world of spirits is one world, even as the world of mortals is one world. We live and act in a world today wherein we find saints and sinners in one sphere; the degraded and defiled, as well as the pious and the pure go about their business on the very same stage of the mortal drama. So it is in the world hereafter—"the spirits of all men, whether they be good or evil" (Alma 40:11), live and move and have their being in one and the same realm. "Where is the spirit world?" Brigham Young asked. He then answered: "It is right here. Do the good and evil spirits go together? Yes, they do. Do they both inhabit one kingdom? Yes, they do."[10] And yet, even as the pure maintain a separate existence from the perverse in this stage of action, so also is there a division between spirits beyond the veil of death. On the one hand, death is a great leveler: it breaks all the bands of poverty, infirmity, and worldly caste or station. On the other hand, death is a great separator, an occasion wherein a "partial judgment" of the spirit results in a designated area of residence. That there was a major separation of the righteous and the wicked before the ministry of the disembodied Savior is evident from the scriptures. (See D&C 138; Luke 16:19–31; 1 Nephi 15:26–30.) Regarding the nature of things since the meridian of time, Heber C. Kimball asked: "Can those persons who pursue a course of carelessness, neglect of duty, and disobedience, when they depart from this life, expect that their spirits will associate with the spirits of the righteous in the spirit world? I do not expect it, and when you depart from this state of existence, you will find it out for yourselves."[11]

A Place of Rest

After teaching his son Corianton concerning the journey of spirits—righteous and wicked—into the spirit world, Alma continued: "And then shall it come to pass, that the spirits of those who are righteous are received into a state of happiness, which is called *paradise, a state of rest, a state of peace,* where they shall rest from all their troubles and from all care, and sorrow" (Alma 40:12; italics added). We thus see that paradise is the abode of the righteous in the world of spirits, a "state of happiness," a place hereafter where the spirits of the faithful "expand in wisdom, where they have respite from all their troubles, and where care and sorrow do not annoy."[12] Those things which burdened the obedient—the worldly cares and struggles, the vicissitudes of life—are shed with the physical body. Paradise is a place where the spirit is free to think and act with a renewed capacity and with the vigor and enthusiasm which characterized one in his prime. Though a person does not rest per se from the work associated with the plan of salvation (for, as we shall see in subsequent chapters, that labor goes forward with at least an equal intensity in the spirit world), at the same time he is delivered from those cares and worries associated with a fallen world and a corrupt body.

The Meaning of "Spirit Prison"

One of the marvelous contributions of President Joseph F. Smith's Vision of the Redemption of the Dead is the heightened realization that the whole spirit world—paradise included—is a "spirit prison." The dead, having "looked upon the long absence of their spirits from their bodies as a bondage," are, in a sense, in prison; they seek redemption and "deliverance" from the "chains of death"; the Master thus came to declare "liberty to the captives who had been faithful." (D&C 138:50, 15, 18.)[13] "When our spirits leave these bodies, will they be happy?" Orson Pratt asked. "Not perfectly so," he responded. "Why? Because the spirit is absent from the body; it cannot be perfectly happy while a part of the man is lying in the earth. . . . You will be happy, you will be at ease in paradise; but still you will be looking for a house where your spirit can enter and act as you did in former times."[14] Brigham Young was most emphatic on this matter: "I know it is a startling idea to say that the Prophet [Joseph Smith] and the persecutor of the Prophet, all go to prison together . . . but *they have not got their bodies yet, consequently they are in prison.*"[15] The doctrine that the entire spirit world is a spirit prison is evident in a marvelous vision given to Enoch. Enoch "looked and beheld the Son of Man lifted up on the cross, after the manner of men; and he heard a loud voice; and the heavens were veiled; and all the creations of God mourned; and the earth groaned; and the rocks were rent; *and the saints arose,* and were crowned at the right hand of the Son of Man, with crowns of glory; and *as many of the spirits as were in prison came forth, and stood on the right hand of God;* and the remainder were reserved in chains of darkness until the judgment of the great day" (Moses 7:55–57; italics added). We note from Enoch's words that *the Saints* were the ones who came forth from the grave. This was the beginning of the first resurrection, the resurrection of the prophets and those who gave heed to the warnings of the prophets (see Mosiah 15:22). These came forth *from prison*—in this instance, from paradise, the abode of the righteous.[16]

Jesus and the Thief on the Cross

One of the most misunderstood biblical passages in Christian history is the account of the Savior's discussion with the thief on the cross during the closing moments of

our Lord's mortal existence. Luke records: "And one of the
malefactors which were hanged railed on [Jesus], saying, If
thou be Christ, save thyself and us. But the other answering
rebuked him, saying, Dost not thou fear God, seeing thou art
in the same condemnation? And we indeed justly; for we
receive the due reward of our deeds: but this man hath done
nothing amiss. And he said unto Jesus, Lord, remember me
when thou comest into thy kingdom. And Jesus said unto
him, Verily I say unto thee, *To day shalt thou be with me in
paradise.*" (Luke 23:39–43; italics added.) This account has
spawned a whole host of incorrect doctrinal perceptions,
which in turn have resulted in questionable and perverse
practices on the part of Christians over the centuries.

One of the most prevalent misperceptions of the above
New Testament dialogue is a belief in a type of "deathbed
repentance," a notion that one can postpone his confession
of the Lord, an acknowledgment of his divine Sonship, and
the outward fruits of one's conversion until the time just
before death. Though we must never de-emphasize or deni-
grate the value of sincere repentance—no matter how late in
one's earthly career (see Matthew 20:1–16)—yet the word of
the Lord is clear that "he that repents *and does the commandments* of the Lord shall be forgiven" (D&C 1:32; italics
added). "Not every one that saith unto me, Lord, Lord, shall
enter into the kingdom of heaven," the Master taught in
time's meridian, "but he that doeth the will of my Father
which is in heaven" (Matthew 7:21). Confession and repentance coerced by the threat of death hardly prepare one's
soul for a place with the sanctified.

There is yet a deeper insight to be had in grasping the
Savior's intended message to the thief on the cross. In dis-
coursing upon the subject, the Prophet Joseph Smith
observed:

> I will say something about the spirits in prison. There has
> been much said by modern divines about the words of Jesus
> (when on the cross) to the thief, saying, "This day shalt thou
> be with me in paradise." King James' translators make it [the
> Greek word *hades*] out to say paradise. But what is paradise? It

is a modern word: it does not answer at all to the original word that Jesus made use of. Find the original of the word paradise. You may as easily find a needle in a haymow. Here is a chance for battle, ye learned men. There is nothing in the original word in Greek from which this was taken that signifies paradise; but it was—*This day thou shalt be with me in the world of spirits.*[17]

In confirming these truths, Joseph Smith said: "Hades, the Greek, Sheol, the Hebrew, these two significations mean a world of spirits. *Hades, Sheol, spirits in prison, are all one: it is a world of spirits.*"[18] Not discounting in any way, therefore, what feelings of contrition may have existed in the heart of the thief on the cross, Parley P. Pratt thus explained that this man went into the world of spirits "in a state of ignorance, and sin, being uncultivated, unimproved, and unprepared for salvation. He went there to be taught, and to complete that repentance, which in a dying moment he commenced on the earth."[19]

A Place of Instruction

Without doubt, the most important work in the world of spirits is the teaching of the gospel. Before the final day of judgment, all must be extended an opportunity to hear the message of salvation from a legal administrator. It is this work of gospel instruction beyond the grave which allows all men to "be judged according to men in the flesh, but live in the spirit according to the will of God" (JST 1 Peter 4:6). Because the primary function of the spirit world is instructional in nature, several of the chapters which follow will focus specifically upon this matter.

A Place of Sorrow and Repentance

Hell

In speaking to Corianton of the second division within the spirit world—that which the scriptures designate as hell or "outer darkness"[20]—Alma said: "And then shall it come to pass, that the spirits of the wicked, yea, who are evil—for behold, they have no part nor portion of the Spirit of the Lord; for behold, they chose evil works rather than good; therefore the spirit of the devil did enter into them, and take possession of their house—and these shall be cast out into outer darkness; there shall be weeping, and wailing, and gnashing of teeth, and this because of their own iniquity, being led captive by the will of the devil" (Alma 40:13). Joseph Smith explained: "The great misery of departed spirits in the world of spirits, where they go after death, is to know that they come short of the glory that others enjoy and that they might have enjoyed themselves, and they are their own accusers."[21] On another occasion, Joseph taught: "A man is his own tormenter and his own condemner. Hence the saying, They shall go into the lake that burns with fire and brimstone. The torment of disappointment in the mind of man is as exquisite as a lake burning with fire and brimstone. I say, so is the torment of man."[22] Thus hell is both a *place*—a part of the world of spirits where suffering and sorrow take place—and a *state*—a condition of the mind associated with remorseful realization. King Benjamin explained that if a man does not repent, "and remaineth and dieth an enemy to God, the demands of divine justice do awaken his immortal soul to a lively sense of his own guilt, which doth cause him to shrink from the presence of the Lord, and doth fill his breast with guilt, and pain, and anguish, which is like an unquenchable fire, whose flame ascendeth up forever and ever" (Mosiah 2:38; cf. Alma 36:12–16).

Nephi foretold the time when people would doubt the reality of the devil as well as the reality of hell. After describing how Satan in the last days would rage in the hearts of some men while pacifying others, he noted: "And behold, others he flattereth away, and telleth them there is no hell; and he saith unto them: I am no devil, for there is none— and thus he whispereth in their ears, until he grasps them with his awful chains, from whence there is no deliverance" (2 Nephi 28:22).[23]

The Law of Restoration

Death does not change the nature of man. The Book of Mormon affirms the principle that man takes into the next sphere of existence that personality and those attitudes which he has cultivated on earth. Just as we come to earth with tendencies and predispositions developed in the premortal world, so also do we go into the afterworld with the character we have shaped and molded in mortality. Were it not so, there would be little purpose in earth life. If we die with desires for goodness and a yearning for righteousness and are questing for the things of the Spirit, we will continue to do so hereafter among those with like propensities. On the other hand, we need not suppose that a lifetime of evil thinking and malevolent motives will be removed or peeled away by the veil of death. Amulek stressed the need for repentance in this life when he said:

> For behold, this life is the time for men to prepare to meet God; yea, behold the day of this life is the day for men to perform their labors.
>
> And now, as I said unto you before, as ye have had so many witnesses, therefore, I beseech of you that ye do not procrastinate the day of your repentance until the end; for after this day of life, which is given us to prepare for eternity, behold, if we do not improve our time while in this life, then cometh the night of darkness wherein there can be no labor performed.
>
> Ye cannot say, when ye are brought to that awful crisis, that I will repent, that I will return to my God. Nay, ye cannot say this; for that same spirit [disposition, attitude] which doth possess your bodies at the time that ye go out of this life, that same spirit will have power to possess your [spirit] body in that eternal world.
>
> For behold, if ye have procrastinated the day of your repentance even until death, behold, ye have become subjected to the spirit of the devil, and he doth seal you his; therefore, the Spirit of the Lord hath withdrawn from you, and hath no place in you, and the devil hath all power over you; and this is the final state of the wicked. (Alma 34:32–35; cf. 41:3–4, 12–13)

Elder Melvin J. Ballard declared: "A man may receive the priesthood and all its privileges and blessings, but until he learns to overcome the flesh—his temper, his tongue, his disposition to indulge in the things God has forbidden—he cannot come into the celestial kingdom of God." In further stressing the importance of bringing about changes in our natures in this life, Elder Ballard continued: "He must overcome either in this life or in the life to come. But this life is the time in which men are to repent. *Do not let any of us imagine that we can go down to the grave not having overcome the corruptions of the flesh and then lose in the grave all our sins and evil tendencies. They will be with us. They will be with the spirit when separated from the body.*" Finally: "Then every man and woman who is putting off until the next life the task of correcting and overcoming the weakness of the flesh are sentencing themselves to years of bondage, for *no man or woman will come forth in the resurrection until he has completed his work, until he has overcome,* until he has done as much as he can do."[24] All who inherit a kingdom of glory will thus have earned the right through appropriate repentance. To be saved in any degree of glory presupposes eventual compliance with the principle of obedience.

A Place of Waiting

The Great Gulf

From the days of Adam until the ministry of the disembodied Savior, there was no link between paradise and hell. Persons who had chosen to follow the ways of the world remained without gospel light for those centuries, and a "great gulf" separated the wicked from the righteous in the world of spirits. "Oh! the weariness, the tardy movement of time!" said Parley P. Pratt, "the lingering ages for a people to dwell in condemnation, darkness, ignorance, and despondency, as a punishment for their sins. For," he noted, "they had been filled with violence while on the earth in the flesh, and had rejected the preachings of . . . the prophets.[25]

The parable of the rich man and Lazarus has often been cited as evidence of such a division in the spirit world. The rich man, finding himself in hell and seeing Lazarus some distance away in the bosom of Abraham—in paradise—cried out for Abraham to send Lazarus, "that he may dip the tip of his finger in water, and cool my tongue; for I am tormented in this flame." Abraham explained that the law of restoration was in full operation—that "thou in thy lifetime receivest thy good things, and likewise Lazarus evil things: but now he is comforted, and thou art tormented. And beside all this," Abraham continued, *"between us and you there is a great gulf fixed: so that they which would pass from hence to you cannot; neither can they pass to us, that would come from thence."* (Luke 16:19–26; italics added.) In commenting specifically upon this parable, Elder Bruce R. McConkie observed that these two men "knew each other in mortality, so they remember their former acquaintance-ship. But no longer are they accessible to each other so that one might minister to the needs of the other. *Christ [had] not bridged the gulf between the prison and the palace, and there [was] as yet no communion between the righteous in paradise and the wicked in hell."* [26]

Nephi, six hundred years earlier, in speaking to his brothers of their father's dream, and particularly of the "fountain of filthy waters," said, *"It [the fountain] was an awful gulf, which separated the wicked from the tree of life, and also from the saints of God."* Nephi further explained that "it was a representation of that awful hell, which the angel said unto me was prepared for the wicked." (1 Nephi 15:28–29; italics added.)

Jesus Christ bridged the gulf between the righteous and the wicked in the spirit world when he visited that realm between the time of his death and resurrection. According to the vision given to Joseph F. Smith, our Lord's ministry to the disembodied was as much organizational as instructional: he preached the gospel to the righteous in paradise and organized them into a force sufficient to carry the message of peace to the wicked, "unto whom he could not go personally, because of their rebellion and transgression" (see

D&C 138:20–37). After the visit of the Savior to those in this segment of spirit prison, the righteous could deliver the soothing waters of eternal life to those in the desert of darkness.[27]

The Ministry of Translated Beings

Because the gospel was not taken to those outside paradise until the meridian of time, the Lord chose periodically to utilize the services of the ancients elsewhere. Many of the righteous were translated—prolonged in life, raised to a terrestrial level of existence, and given assignments to continue their labors in behalf of the children of men. In speaking of Enoch and his city, the Prophet Joseph Smith stated, "Their place of habitation is that of the terrestrial order, and a place prepared for such characters He held in reserve to be ministering angels unto many planets."[28] When the gulf was bridged in the postmortal world, this practice changed. "Occasionally in the overall perspective someone came along who so lived that he was translated, but that's not particularly for our day and generation. When we die our obligation is to go into the spirit world and to continue to preach the gospel there."[29]

A Place of Reunion

For the righteous, the time of death is also a time of reunion, an occasion wherein a person is welcomed once again to the society of loved ones. "I have a father, brothers, children, and friends who have gone to a world of spirits," Joseph Smith said in 1844. "They are only absent for a moment. They are in the spirit, and we shall soon meet again."[30] President Joseph F. Smith asked: "What is more desirable than that we should meet with our fathers and our mothers, with our brethren and our sisters, with our wives and our children, with our beloved associates and kindred in the spirit world, knowing each other, identifying each other . . . by the associations that familiarize each to the other in mortal life? What do you want better than that? What is there for any religion superior to that? I know of nothing."[31] Relationships are among the most significant developments of this life. Such bonds may be infinite and eternal, and the phenomenon of death merely interrupts these ties. The entry into the spirit world at the time of one's passing provides a glorious opportunity for renewal and perpetuation of associations.

Conclusion

The restoration of the gospel through the instrumentality of Joseph Smith has opened the doors of understanding to things both seen and unseen. To those who are willing to enter the realm of knowledge and bask in the living light made available through modern revelation and modern oracles, there is an infinitude of intelligence available concerning the continuation of life after death, of existence beyond this sphere. Truth—glorious truth—proclaims that life did not begin at mortal birth, nor will it end at mortal death. Our development and progress did not begin as we first breathed the breath of life, nor will it cease when we breathe our last. Life goes on—in a world of spirits, beyond the grave.

3

That All Might Hear

Wherefore the voice of the Lord is unto the ends of the earth,
that all that will hear may hear.

—D&C 1:11

What of gospel principles beyond death? What of mercy and justice? What of faith and repentance? of ritual and ordinance? Having served their functions in mortality, are they then, like the body of man, consigned to the dust of the earth? What of those who spurn the saving word in the flesh but thereafter thirst for a drop of living water? And what of those who left mortality having never felt the warmth of gospel light? Or those from whom blessings and promises were withheld because of circumstances beyond their control? What of those who received less than a wholeness here—what is their hope for a fulness hereafter? Is there order in heaven, a divine plan, a plan reaching from eternity to eternity? On matters of such infinite import the revealed word is not silent.

A World of Confusion or a House of Order?

The theologies of the world are a mass of confusion. They evidence the apostasy and attest to the puniness of the mind of man when unaided by the Spirit of God. They lack mercy and are devoid of justice, for they portray a God with power to save but a portion of his creatures, and that too on an inequitable basis. They are founded in uncertainty and some even in ambiguity. They deny revelation and yet in their doctrines freely add to the scriptural canon. Some promise salvation to the wicked and faithless by grace alone; others damn innocent and pure children. But the Latter-day Saint reader ought to be reminded that without a divine dispensation we would be no better informed than our friends from other churches. Were it not for the restoration of the gospel and the advent of living prophets, our understanding would reach no higher than theirs.

The God of heaven is a God of order. He is a God perfect in mercy and flawless in justice, as with all other attributes of godliness. The divine and eternal truths which flow from him, like their author, are without fault. As all men have equal claim upon his attentions and his love, so all men are equally entitled to inherit and possess the blessings that come from obedience to his precepts and commands. A God of justice could not consign one to heaven on the basis of the good fortune of having been born in the presence of legal authorities, those who can perform the ordinances essential to salvation, while consigning another to hell because he was not so well born. A religion that cannot offer salvation to Abraham, Isaac, and Jacob because they lived before Christ, or that cannot save the newly born infant that died in perfect innocence, can make no honest profession to represent a God of either mercy or justice. Such theology does not differ in principle from one that would offer salvation to those afforded the opportunity to make a deathbed profession of faith, while damning those to whom no such opportunity came.

The Bible, notwithstanding the many marvelous truths it contains, can be searched in vain for the simple affirmation that our Eternal Father has a *plan* for the salvation of his children. The misunderstanding and confusion in the world is not without justification. It is an eternal verity that it takes prophets to understand prophets and the spirit of revelation to properly understand those revelations already given. The understanding we as Latter-day Saints have of the "plan of salvation" would not be ours were it not for the Book of Mormon and other revelations of the Restoration. Phrases like "merciful plan of the great Creator" (2 Nephi 9:6), "eternal plan of deliverance" (2 Nephi 11:5), "great plan of redemption" (Jacob 6:8), and "plan of salvation" (Alma 24:14) are common to the Book of Mormon.

Though our modern Bible contains no references to a plan of salvation, anciently it was not so. We are primarily indebted to the writings of Abraham and Moses for our understanding of the pre-earth life and the Grand Council in Heaven, at which our Eternal Father reviewed his plan for the salvation of his children. Scriptural references to the heavenly council are at best brief. The terseness in which they are given, even in the books of Moses and Abraham, is an evidence that they were common knowledge to those to whom they were originally given. Details were not necessary, for the doctrine was well known. Peter's reference to Christ's visit to the spirit world illustrates the point: these verses are not the result of a discourse on the subject; they are simply a succinct illustration used in making some other point.

Abraham's revelation, for instance, first announces that the souls of all men lived in the presence of their Eternal Father prior to their birth into mortality. Further, it tells us that judgments were made among their number as to which were the most noble and faithful, for these were singled out and foreordained to be leaders in the kingdom of God. Abraham was told that he was one of those so chosen. Finally, in this Grand Council the God of heaven asked of the assembled spirits, "Whom shall I send?" meaning: "Whom shall I choose to be the Savior or Redeemer of mankind?" The question implies that those being addressed understood the necessity of a Redeemer in the divine plan. (See Abraham 3:18–28.) The eldest or firstborn of this great family of spirits responded to the question, saying, "Here am I, send me." To Abraham's account Moses adds these words: "Father, thy will be done, and the glory be thine forever" (Moses 4:2). This response assumes significance only if the Son understood the will of the Father and how the Son's obedience to that divine will would bring the Father glory.

We see then that Jesus' role as the Savior of mankind can properly be understood only in the context of the Father's plan for the salvation of his children. It is of considerable significance that our Heavenly Father did not attempt to raise his children without a plan and that the plan required them to assemble as a family council. Of necessity that plan embraced the following elements:

1. An earth had to be created, one to which God's spirit children could come to obtain physical bodies, the physical body being a requisite to godhood.

2. In its creation, the earth would be paradisiacal, meaning there would be no death or corruption on it. All forms of life were to be placed on the earth but not granted the power of procreation as long as the earth remained in its Edenic state. Those chosen to be our first parents would have to transgress the laws of that paradisiacal state in order to have children. It would then become possible for them and their posterity to be tried and tested to see if they would merit the privilege of returning to the presence of their Divine Father. That transgression, known to us as the fall of Adam, introduced death, corruption, and sin. In this state of corruption, Adam and his posterity could no longer enjoy the presence of the Lord and thus would be known as fallen man.

3. The effects of Adam's fall could only be overcome by an atoning sacrifice made by one free from the effects of sin. The Redeemer must have within his nature both the ability to lay down his life and the power to take it up again. By so doing he could atone for the sins of the world, break the bands of death, and bring to pass a resurrection (the inseparable union of body and spirit).

4. Thus, the one chosen to redeem mankind from the effects of the fall must have God as his father—from whom he could inherit the capacity to live endlessly—and a mortal mother, from whom he could inherit blood or the corruptible element of the body, so that he might die. As the Only Begotten of the Father in the flesh, he would then be able to lay down his life in an atoning sacrifice and take it up again, thus breaking the bands of death.

5. As all would be subject to death by Adam's transgression, so all could be freed from its bondage by Christ's atonement. All would be granted the opportunity to accept Christ as their Savior and work out their salvation by complying with the laws and ordinances of the gospel. Those not having the opportunity to do so in mortality were to be granted that opportunity in the world of the spirits prior to the resurrection.

6. Thus, all men in all ages of earth's history would be invited to follow the same path, exercise the same faith, comply with the same ordinances, and live the same principles in order to be saved in the kingdom of God.

A Gospel for All Peoples

A Gospel for All Mankind

The gospel and its blessings are intended for all mankind. In the meridian of time Peter declared, "God is no respecter of persons: But in *every nation* he that feareth him, and worketh righteousness, is accepted with him" (Acts 10:34–35; italics added). Reflecting this same principle in our dispensation, Joseph Smith wrote, "We believe that through the Atonement of Christ, *all mankind* may be saved, by obedience to the laws and ordinances of the Gospel" (Articles of Faith 1:3; italics added). The salvation which is gained by obedience to the laws and ordinances of the gospel means an inheritance of eternal life or the obtaining of exaltation. As an illustration, we have a revelation that reads, "If thou wilt do good, yea, and hold out faithful to the end, thou shalt be saved in the kingdom of God, which is the *greatest of all the gifts of God; for there is no gift greater than the gift of salvation"* (D&C 6:13; italics added). Similarly, Joseph Smith taught that *"salvation consists in the glory, authority, majesty, power and dominion which Jehovah possesses and in nothing else."* [1]

The Gospel and Its Blessings Are for All Races

The gospel and its blessings are to go to all races, nations, and lineages before the Second Coming. John foresaw that an angelic ministrant would bring again "the everlasting gospel to preach unto them that dwell on the earth, and *to every nation, and kindred, and tongue, and people"* (Revelation 14:6; italics added). Of the gospel restored through Joseph Smith the Lord said: "And this gospel *shall* be preached unto *every nation, and kindred, and tongue, and people"* (D&C 133:37; italics added).

There are numerous revelations commanding us to preach the gospel to "every creature" (D&C 18:28; 58:64; 80:1; 84:62; 112:28–30; 124:128). One of these says, "Go ye into all the world, preach the gospel to *every creature,"* and then with reference to those who believe and obey, says, "to you shall be given power to *seal them up unto eternal life"* (D&C 68:8–12; italics added). To be sealed up unto eternal life includes the receipt of temple ordinances.

John saw in vision that all of this would take place before the Millennium. He saw those who had been "redeemed . . . of *every kindred, and tongue, and people, and nation,"* and wrote that they were the ones who would "reign on the earth" with Christ (Revelation 5:9–10; italics added). "They shall be priests of God and of Christ, and shall reign with him a thousand years" (Revelation 20:6). Thus, before the Millennium, we must make converts from every kindred and tongue and people and nation, and they must progress in spiritual things until they receive the Melchizedek Priesthood and the ordinances of the house of the Lord.

The Family of Abraham

All those who receive the gospel become members of the family of Abraham and are entitled to all of the blessings of the gospel. Jehovah told Abraham that his seed would take the gospel and the *"Priesthood unto all nations,"* and that "as many as receive this Gospel shall be called after thy name, and shall be accounted thy seed, and shall rise up and bless thee, as their father." These are adopted into the house of Israel. Jehovah also promised Abraham that when his literal seed took the message of salvation to *"all nations"* then "shall *all the families of the earth* be blessed, even with *the blessings of the Gospel,* which are the blessings *of salvation, even of life eternal."* (Abraham 2:9–11; italics added.)

The Promise to Abraham's Seed Reaches Beyond the Veil

"Abraham, Isaac, and Jacob—and their seed—have the natural right (such is the promise given them of God) to the priesthood, the gospel, and a fulness of salvation, which is eternal life! And this includes all of 'the literal seed, or the seed of the body,' whether they lived when the gospel was on the earth or not!"[2] Death does not dissolve the promises and covenants of God. Teaching the gospel in the world of spirits is inherent in the Abrahamic covenant.

The vision of the degrees of glory, like the book of Isaiah, begins by saying: "Hear, O ye heavens, and give ear, O earth" (D&C 76:1; Isaiah 1:2). Commenting on such verses, Bruce R. McConkie said: "In other words . . . the Lord was announcing truth to heaven and to earth because those principles of salvation operate on both sides of the veil; and salvation is administered to an extent here to men, and it is administered to another extent in the spirit world. We correlate and combine our activities and do certain things for the salvation of men while we are in mortality, and then certain things are done for the salvation of men while they are in the spirit world awaiting the day of the resurrection."[3]

A classic illustration of this principle in our modern day is the revelation received in June 1978, which extended the priesthood and the full blessings of the house of the Lord to those of all races. At the present point in time there may well be appreciably greater numbers of people prepared to receive these blessings on the other side of the veil than there are presently in mortality.

No Unearned Blessings

How the Lord Taught Salvation for the Dead to Joseph Smith

To most clearly understand the principles of salvation for the dead we must learn them as the Lord taught them to the Prophet Joseph Smith. We must lay the right foundation and then carefully build the house of our understanding brick by brick. Joseph Smith learned the gospel from the Book of Mormon. In the process of translating the gold plates, Joseph was required to struggle with the message of the book thought by thought, concept by concept, doctrine by doctrine. Thus he studiously and prayerfully worked his way through this ancient record, extracting the message from the writings of his fellow prophets, getting it clearly into his own heart and mind, clothing the message in the English language, and seeking the confirmation of the Spirit that his translation was correct. The process was such that the Prophet was tutored or schooled by the voice of these noble souls of ages past.

From Jacob, Joseph learned that God had commanded "all men that they must repent, and be baptized in his name, having perfect faith in the Holy One of Israel, or they cannot be saved in the kingdom of God. And if they will not repent and believe in his name, and be baptized in his name, and endure to the end, they must be damned; for the Lord God, the Holy One of Israel, has spoken it." (2 Nephi 9:23–24.) As Joseph and Oliver Cowdery translated such passages, they recognized this as the voice of the Lord to them. This in turn raised in their minds the question of how they could be baptized and by what authority that ordinance could be performed. As the matter worked itself upon their hearts and minds they interrupted the work of translation to go into the woods, find a secluded spot, and implore the heavens for an answer.[4]

From Amulek, Joseph Smith learned that his religion was to be "a now or never" or "day of this life" religion. In his great discourse to the Zoramites, Amulek forever set to rest the idea of deathbed repentance and the idea that someone could be prayed out of their judgment at death. "Do not procrastinate the day of your repentance until the end," he declared, "for after this day of life, which is given us to prepare for eternity, behold, if we do not improve our time while in this life, then cometh the night of darkness wherein there can be no labor performed." Amulek then explained the reason why the life of spiritual poverty here cannot be one of spiritual wealth hereafter: the spirit is the same. Those who are without faith here will be without faith there; those without the desire or propensity for righteousness here will be without them there. We go into the world of the spirits as the sum of what we have become here, nothing more and nothing less. (Alma 34:33–34.)

Amulek's testimony is echoed throughout the Book of Mormon. Samuel applied the principle to the wicked and rebellious of his day, saying, "Your days of probation are past; ye have procrastinated the day of your salvation until it is everlastingly too late, and your destruction is made sure" (Helaman 13:38). Christ invited the righteous remnants of the Nephite nation to come unto him and be saved, saying, "For verily I say unto you, that except ye shall keep my commandments, which I have commanded you *at this time,* ye shall in no case enter into the kingdom of heaven (3 Nephi 12:20; italics added).

We see, then, that it was absolutely imperative that Joseph Smith learn that the opportunities and responsibilities of this life are paramount in the working out of one's salvation. Never has a doctrine come from the heavens that excuses disobedience or spiritual lethargy in any form. The Prophet had to clearly understand this before the Lord would even hint at the possibility of a doctrine of salvation for the dead.

Joseph Smith's Vision of the Celestial Kingdom

It was almost six years after the organization of the Church, 21 January 1836, that Joseph Smith first learned that those who died without the gospel in this life might receive its blessings in the spirit world. The revelation came while Joseph Smith, his father the patriarch, and leaders of the Church from Ohio and Missouri were involved in administering the anointing with oil and the giving of special blessings to each other. In the midst of this, Joseph said: "The heavens were opened upon us, and I beheld the celestial kingdom of God, and the glory thereof, whether in the body or out I cannot tell. I saw the transcendent beauty of the gate through which the heirs of that kingdom will enter, which was like unto circling flames of fire; Also the blazing throne of God, whereon was seated the Father and the Son. I saw the beautiful streets of that kingdom, which had the appearance of being paved with gold. I saw Father Adam and Abraham; and my father and my mother; my brother Alvin, that has long since slept; And marveled how it was that he had obtained an inheritance in that kingdom, seeing that he had departed this life before the Lord had set his hand to gather Israel the second time, and had not been baptized for the remission of sins." (D&C 137:1–6.)

To have the heavens opened was not a new experience to Joseph. No surprise is manifest at such a happening. Nor was the seeing of the Father and the Son a novel experience, for he had had such experiences before (Joseph Smith—History 1:17; D&C 76:22–24). To see Adam and Abraham merits no special mention by him. The sight of his father and mother in the heavenly vision also seemed to have been most natural to his understanding. On the other hand, the sight of his older brother Alvin caused him to *marvel*. Why? Because Alvin died before John the Baptist restored the

Aaronic Priesthood and the authority to perform legal and binding baptisms.

From Joseph's response to this vision we know that by 21 January 1836 the idea of teaching the gospel in the spirit world and the performance of vicarious ordinances had not occurred to him. It was at this point that the Lord, building on the theological foundation laid in the "day of this life" doctrine of the Book of Mormon, chose to lift the veil and expand our understanding of the justice of God and the marvels of the plan of salvation. "Thus came the voice of the Lord unto me," Joseph said, "All who have died without a knowledge of this gospel, who would have received it if they had been permitted to tarry, shall be heirs of the celestial kingdom of God; Also all that shall die henceforth without a knowledge of it, who would have received it with all their hearts, shall be heirs of that kingdom; For I, the Lord, will judge all men according to their works, according to the desire of their hearts" (D&C 137:7–9).

For the first time in revealed word we have announced to us the standards by which one in the world of the spirits can receive the gospel unto exaltation. The promise is not to all, for in the Vision of the Glories we have already been told that the terrestrial kingdom will have among its number those "who received not the testimony of Jesus in the flesh, but afterwards received it" (D&C 76:74). Or, as Joseph Smith stated in his poetic form of that vision, "They received not the truth of the Saviour at first; But did, when they heard it in prison again."[5] Those who can accept the gospel in the world of spirits and be exalted must: (1) have died without the opportunity to have accepted it in his life; (2) be judged of God as being of that disposition that had the opportunity to accept the message come to them in earth life, they would have done so; and (3) having accepted it, they would have done so "with all their hearts," meaning they would have endured in faith to the end. The revelation complies fully with the statement of Peter, that those in the spirit world are to be "judged according to men in the flesh" (1 Peter 4:6). It is a perfect expression of the law of justification or the idea that with the Lord there are no unearned blessings.

Alvin Smith the Perfect Prototype

The truths thus revealed must have been the source of great rejoicing in the Smith family. The passing of Alvin had been a matter of considerable sorrow. Their wounded souls had been cut to the core by the unfeeling and intemperate remarks of the Presbyterian minister who had consigned Alvin to hell at his funeral simply because he had not been baptized or involved in that church.[6]

Despite his relative youth, Alvin was a man of unusual spiritual propensity. Before his death, he called each of his brothers and sisters in turn to his bedside and gave them a parting admonition. To his eighteen-year-old brother Joseph he said: "Be a good boy, and do everything that lies in your power to obtain the Record [having reference to the Book of Mormon]. Be faithful in receiving instruction, and in keeping every commandment that is given you."[7] Mother Smith stated that "Alvin manifested, if such could be the case, greater zeal and anxiety in regard to the Record that had been shown to Joseph, than any of the rest of the family; in consequence of which we could not bear to hear anything said upon the subject. Whenever Joseph spoke of the Record, it would immediately bring Alvin to our minds, with all his zeal, and with all his kindness; and, when we looked to his place, and realized that he was gone from it, to return no more in this life, we all with one accord wept over our irretrievable loss, and we could 'not be comforted because he was not.'"[8]

Nearly twenty years later, Joseph Smith recounted his feelings at the time of Alvin's death, saying: "I remember well the pangs of sorrow that swelled my youthful bosom and almost burst my tender heart when he died. He was the oldest and noblest of my father's family. . . . He lived without spot from the time he was a child. . . . He was one of the soberest of men, and when he died the angel of the Lord visited him in his last moments."[9]

Thus we see Joseph Smith's Vision of the Celestial Kingdom as a most perfect teaching device. Each of the characters seen by the Prophet in the vision are singularly representative: Adam, the father of all, the beginning of the great patriarchal chain; Abraham, the father of the faithful, the great patriarch to whom the promise of an endless seed was given; father Smith and his faithful wife, Lucy Mack, representing the immediate family unit to the mind of Joseph; and his beloved brother Alvin, who had died without the opportunity to embrace the fulness of the gospel and comply with its saving ordinances—these were especially chosen by the providence of heaven to represent visually the principles being taught. From the comments of Joseph and his mother we see Alvin as the perfect illustration of the principles announced in the vision. Though Alvin died without the opportunity to accept the gospel, the works and attitudes of his life were such as to attest that had the opportunity come to him he would have embraced it and would have done so with all his heart.

It ought also to be observed that the vision was not of things as they then were in the celestial realms, but rather a depiction of what they could be. Though seen in the vision, Joseph Sr. and Lucy were still living. Indeed, Joseph's father was present when the vision was received. Joseph Smith Sr. lived for another four years. He passed away 14 September 1840, while Joseph's mother, Lucy Mack Smith, lived for another nineteen years, passing away 5 May 1855.

The Heresy of Salvation for the Dead

When Amulek spoke of death as the "night of darkness wherein there can be no labor performed" (Alma 34:33), he had reference to those who had full opportunity to accept the gospel in the flesh and did not do so. It is a serious doctrinal error to suppose that those who reject that opportunity in this life because they have no desire to conform to gospel standards may correct the matter in the spirit world. The willfully disobedient will not be cleansed from their sins simply because they have the good fortune to have someone labor in their behalf after they are dead. The book of life from which each man will be judged will be the book he has written on his own soul.

No Blessings Denied the Worthy

The law of justification, which holds on the one hand that there are no unearned blessings, that no one is going to slip into the kingdom of heaven using the back door or on someone else's coattail, also extends in the other direction. The promise is that, from one end of eternity to another, every righteous man or woman who did not receive a certain blessing because of circumstances beyond his or her control will have the opportunity to receive those blessings in the world to come. For instance, those who did not have the opportunity to be baptized, to be endowed, to be married in the temple, to have children, or to receive any other blessing, because of circumstances beyond their control, will have those blessings offered to them. Such is the justice of God, and such is the glory of the gospel. Standing alone, the principle is sufficient to testify of the truthfulness of the restored gospel and witness that Joseph Smith was and is a prophet. The world, for all its wisdom, cannot match such principles.

Conclusion

In the great revelation announcing the opening of this, the last gospel dispensation, it is stated that *"the voice of the Lord is unto the ends of the earth, that all that will hear may hear"* (D&C 1:11; italics added). Further, the Lord said: "That these things might be known among you, O inhabitants of the earth, I have sent forth mine angel flying through the midst of heaven, having the everlasting gospel, who hath appeared unto some and hath committed it unto man, who shall appear unto many that dwell on the earth. And this gospel shall be preached unto every nation, and kindred, and tongue, and people." (D&C 133:36–37.) And then by way of further amplification the Lord said, "And this shall be the sound of his trump, saying to all people, both in heaven and in earth, *and that are under the earth* [meaning those in the spirit world]—for every ear shall hear it, and every knee shall bow, and every tongue shall confess, while they hear the sound of the trump, saying: Fear God, and give glory to him who sitteth upon the throne, forever and ever; for the hour of his judgment is come" (D&C 88:104; italics added).

4

The Gospel: Here and Hereafter

For for this cause was the gospel preached also to them that are dead, that they might be judged according to men in the flesh, but live according to God in the spirit.

—1 Peter 4:6

As gospel principles are everlastingly and eternally the same, so is the manner in which they are taught. As faith comes in this life by hearing the word of God through the spirit of revelation, so it comes in the world hereafter. As God calls prophets here, he calls them there; as he clothes his servants with power and authority here, he likewise clothes them there; as he sends forth missionaries to every nation and kindred on earth, so all within the world of spirits will be granted like opportunity. As the gospel is taught to congregation and individual here, so it is taught in that future world. With the restoration of the gospel to earth has come the knowledge that the gospel is taught beyond the bounds of mortality, the knowledge of how it is taught, and the knowledge of the role the faithful will yet play in teaching it.

Opening the Prison to Them That Are Bound

Having established his Church in the meridian of time, Christ then promised that the "gates of hell" would not prevail against it. He promised Peter the "keys of the kingdom," explaining that these keys contained the authority by which those things bound on earth would also be bound in heaven, and those things loosed on earth would be loosed in heaven. (See Matthew 16:18–19.) The meaning of this promise has remained an enigma to the Christian world, one which becomes clear only through the restoration of those same keys and by the same instruction being given to modern prophets that was conferred upon Peter and the meridian Twelve.

The term *keys* symbolizes power and authority. Specifically, it signifies the authority and responsibility to preside in the *kingdom* to which Christ referred, the earthly Church. That kingdom either had just been organized or was about to be. When Christ likened "the kingdom of heaven" to one thing or another in the parables given in Matthew 13, he was essentially saying, "The Church of Jesus Christ is likened to this thing or that." Now, in saying to Peter that he was to be given the *"keys of the kingdom,"* Christ was saying: "You will preside over the Church and all ordinances performed in it. They must be done under your direction and by your permission in order to be of 'efficacy, virtue, or force' in and after men are dead. Thus, that which you approve will be binding in the worlds to come and that which you loose or dissolve will be of no effect in the worlds to come." Describing this same authority as it was restored to Joseph Smith, the Lord said, "Whatsoever you seal on earth shall be sealed in heaven; and whatsoever you bind on earth, in my name and by my word, saith the Lord, it shall be eternally bound in the heavens; and whosesoever sins you remit on earth shall be remitted eternally in the heavens; and whosesoever sins you retain on earth shall be retained in heaven" (D&C 132:46).

Peter, then, was given an authority against which the "gates of hell" could not prevail. Gates are used to keep things in a confined area or to keep other things out. A gate has prevailed when it has accomplished that purpose. *Hell,* in this instance, has reference to the world of the spirits.

The Savior's promise to Peter included: (1) the

announcement that he would preside over the Church and kingdom of God on earth; (2) the granting of the responsibility to preside over all the ordinances of salvation—that which he approved on earth being approved in heaven, and that which he nullified on earth being null and void in heaven; and (3) the authority to preside over the Church in the world of the spirits, in which he could open and close the gates of salvation to those in the world of spirits to whom the opportunity to accept or reject the gospel had not come in this life.

Each of these promises was for an authority that Peter would yet receive. Obviously he would not preside over the earthly Church while the Savior was still with them, nor would he preside over its counterpart in the world of the spirits until his earthly ministry was finished and his spirit departed from its tabernacle of clay. Nor would we suppose that Peter fully understood the implications of the Savior's promise when it was first given in Caesarea Philippi. Much instruction and explanation was yet needed. For the most part, that instruction would be given Peter and the Twelve after the Savior's resurrection in what we know as the forty-day ministry.

The keys of which Christ had spoken were conferred upon Peter, James, and John—the First Presidency of the Church—the following week on what is known as the Mount of Transfiguration (see Matthew 17:1–13).[1] Those same keys were conferred upon the others of the Twelve by Christ on the eve of his resurrection while they were assembled in the upper room (see John 20:22–23). Thus, the Twelve now held those keys containing the authority to prevail or preside even over the "gates of hell." The stage was now set to teach them the nature of missionary work in the spirit world and the necessity of vicarious ordinances being performed on earth for those who accepted the gospel in the world of the spirits.

The Testimony of Bible Prophets

The Bible does not detail the manner in which the gospel is to be preached in the spirit world. This is not a doctrine known to the world. As noted in the second chapter, the idea that there is an intermediate state—a place in which departed spirits await the time of resurrection and the day of judgment—is not a part of traditional Christian theology. Yet scattered throughout the Bible are sufficient references to the nature of these events that the informed reader need have no doubt that they were known to and understood by the ancient prophets.

In a great messianic prophecy, Isaiah announced that Christ would "proclaim liberty to the captives," and that he would open "the prison to them that are bound" (Isaiah 61:1). In his mortal ministry, Christ said: "The hour is coming, and now is, when the dead shall hear the voice of the Son of God: and they that hear shall live. For as the Father hath life in himself; so hath he given to the Son to have life in himself; And hath given him authority to execute judgment also, because he is the Son of man. Marvel not at this: for the hour is coming, in the which all that are in the graves shall hear his voice, and shall come forth; they that have done good, unto the resurrection of life; and they that have done evil, unto the resurrection of damnation." (John 5:25–29.) Peter taught that after Christ had been "put to death in the flesh" he would be "quickened by the Spirit" and would preach "unto the spirits in prison," among them those who "were disobedient, when once the longsuffering of God waited in the days of Noah." Thus they would be granted the opportunity to hear the word of God preached in the spirit world. (JST 1 Peter 3:18–20.)

Organizing a Mission in the Spirit World

Without question, the greatest revelation on the nature of missionary work in the spirit world is Joseph F. Smith's Vision of the Redemption of the Dead, now found in section 138 of the Doctrine and Covenants. From this revelation we learn that while his body lay in the borrowed tomb of Joseph of Arimathea, Christ, "quickened by the Spirit," joined a great assembly of faithful Saints in the paradise of God. Apparently they were assembled in a conference of the Church, a meeting patterned after the great conference that Adam held with the righteous residue of his posterity in the valley of Adam-ondi-Ahman. There Adam presided until Christ appeared to instruct and bless them. (See D&C 107: 53–55.)

Among the unnumbered host in this great conference in the spirit world surrounding Adam and his faithful wife, Eve, were Abel, Seth, Noah, Shem, Abraham, Isaac, Jacob, Moses, Isaiah, Ezekiel, Daniel, Elijah, and Malachi from the old world, with Lehi, Nephi, Jacob, and a host of prophets and righteous souls from among the Nephites. All thus assembled had departed mortal life firm in the faith. Each had worshiped the Father in the name of the Son. Each had participated in the offering of sacrifices in similitude of the atoning sacrifice of Christ. Though they had been persecuted for their faith, they esteemed it an honor "to suffer tribulation in their Redeemer's name." The spirit of the meeting was one of rejoicing and gladness as they awaited the arrival of the Savior and anticipated the resurrection and glories that would be theirs.

Thus we read: "While this vast multitude waited and conversed, rejoicing in the hour of their deliverance from the chains of death, the Son of God appeared, declaring liberty to the captives who had been faithful; and there he preached to them the everlasting gospel, the doctrine of the resurrection and the redemption of mankind from the fall, and from individual sins on conditions of repentance. But unto the wicked he did not go, and among the ungodly and the unrepentant who had defiled themselves while in the flesh, his voice was not raised; neither did the rebellious who rejected the testimonies and the warnings of the ancient prophets behold his presence, nor look upon his face. Where these were, darkness reigned, but among the righteous there was peace; and the saints rejoiced in their redemption, and bowed the knee and acknowledged the Son of God as their Redeemer and Deliverer from death and the chains of hell." (D&C 138:18–23.)

Having taught a matchless discourse on gospel essentials, having testified anew to the prophets of old on such matters as the Fall, the Atonement, and the Resurrection, Christ then turned his attention to organizational matters. As noted above, among the wicked and disobedient he would not go in person. It is not the right of such to stand in the presence of the Lord (D&C 138:37). Had the wicked joined the assembly of the righteous, receiving the full benefits therefrom, it could hardly be said of them that they had been judged according to men in the flesh. Rather, our Master and Savior called from among the assembly of the righteous certain of their number to serve as missionaries. These were to take the glorious message of the gospel to those who had died in their sins and those who had died in ignorance of that message. Our key passage states it thus: "But behold, from among the righteous, he *organized* his forces and appointed *messengers,* clothed with *power* and *authority,* and *commissioned* them to go forth and carry the light of the gospel to them that were in darkness, even to all the spirits of men; and thus was the gospel preached to the dead" (D&C 138:30; italics added).

The matter is most enlightening. Here assembled are the great and noble from Adam, who was and is Michael the archangel, to John the Baptist, of whom the Savior said there had not been a greater prophet born of woman. Since the councils of heaven, such a body of valiant teachers had not sat together. And yet of their number not a single soul had supposed the right was his to preach the gospel to those in darkness without the commission of the Lord. They did not want for the knowledge of the gospel, nor did they lack the faith to teach it, but to assume the prerogative to teach without the proper commission was something they would not do. As the house of the Lord is one of discipline and order in this life, so it is on the other side of the veil. As none are to go forth to preach the gospel or build up the Church here without authorization (D&C 42:11), so they are not to do so there.

Again, in all that comes from God there is a sense of discipline and order. As to the teaching of the gospel, there is a divine timetable; all are to hear it, but each in order, each in his appointed time. This is why baptism and other temple ordinances were not performed vicariously during Old Testament times. Not until Christ had organized his missionary forces in the world of the spirits do we find references to the Saints practicing the ordinance of baptism for the dead (1 Corinthians 15:29).

Joseph Smith Now Presides in the Spirit World

"As in earth, so in the spirit world," said Parley P. Pratt. "No person can enter into the privileges of the Gospel, until the keys are turned, and the Gospel opened by those in authority, for all which there is a time, according to the wise dispensations of justice and mercy."[2] The Lord taught this principle to Joseph Smith in this language: "Everything that is in the world, whether it be ordained of men, by thrones, or principalities, or powers, or things of name, whatsoever they may be, that are not by me or by my word, saith the Lord, shall be thrown down, and shall not remain after men are dead, neither in nor after the resurrection, saith the Lord your God. For whatsoever things remain are by me; and whatsoever things are not by me shall be shaken and destroyed." (D&C 132:13–14.)

For the gospel to continue in the spirit world the priesthood must continue in the spirit world. For those holding the priesthood to have the right to function in their priesthood the keys of the priesthood must be present also to direct their labors. Our revelations assure us that this is the case. To Joseph Smith the Lord said, "Verily I say unto you, the keys of this kingdom shall never be taken from you, while thou art in the world, neither in the world to come; nevertheless, through you shall the oracles be given to another, yea, even unto the church" (D&C 90:3–4). Thus, Joseph could confer his keys upon the Twelve so that their powers would not be lost to us when he died, and at the same time he would carry those keys with him to preside over a great gospel dispensation in the spirit world.

Recounting his Vision of the Redemption of the Dead, Joseph F. Smith said:

> I beheld that the faithful elders of this dispensation, when they depart from mortal life, continue their labors in the preaching of the gospel of repentance and redemption, through the sacrifice of the Only Begotten Son of God, among those who are in darkness and under the bondage of sin in the great world of the spirits of the dead.
>
> The dead who repent will be redeemed, through obedience to the ordinances of the house of God,
>
> And after they have paid the penalty of their transgressions, and are washed clean, shall receive a reward according to their works, for they are heirs of salvation. (D&C 138: 57–59.)

President Joseph F. Smith also testified that the teaching of the gospel in the spirit world to those of our dispensation has begun under the direction of Joseph Smith. All the faithful prophets and Apostles of our dispensation are sustaining him in that labor. "They are there," he said, "having carried with them from here the holy Priesthood that they received under authority, and which was conferred upon them in the flesh; they are preaching the gospel to the spirits in prison; for Christ, when his body lay in the tomb, went to proclaim liberty to the captives and opened the prison doors to them that were bound." Then President Smith added, "Not only are these engaged in that work but hundreds and thousands of others," having reference to all the faithful elders of this dispensation.[3]

Nature of the Gospel Taught to the Spirits

Having established that organization and order are as much a part of the gospel plan in the world of the spirits as they are in mortality, let us now turn our attention to the message that the missionaries in the world of spirits were commissioned to declare to those spirits under the bondage of sin and ignorance. "These were taught," we are told, "faith in God, repentance from sin, vicarious baptism for the remission of sins, the gift of the Holy Ghost by the laying on of hands, And all other principles of the gospel that were necessary for them to know in order to qualify themselves that they might be judged according to men in the flesh, but live according to God in the spirit" (D&C 138:33–34). We see, then, that every principle of the gospel has retained its weight and measure in the world of the spirits. All are to be taught as they were on the earth and all principles are to be accepted and lived as they were on the earth. Spirits are to be judged according to men in the flesh, and if the judgment be the same, the principles must of necessity be the same.[4]

How the Gospel Is Taught in the Spirit World

Legal Administrators

As we have heaven-sent standards by which the gospel is to be preached among men on earth, so those standards apply to the teaching of the gospel in the world of the spirits. As we have seen, the gospel must be taught by legal administrators. Prophets of God would not think to arrogate to themselves the right to teach without a divine sanction. Though knowledge, love, sincerity, and zeal are all to be commended, none of these constitute a divine commission. The priesthood is as necessary for the teaching of the gospel in the spirit world as it is in this life. Further, the priesthood does not function independently. The Lord's house is a house of order and his priesthood is a priesthood of order. That authority which disciplines or directs the priesthood is known as the *keys* or the *keys of the kingdom*. All that is to be binding in the world to come must be done by or under the direction of the priesthood, and all that the priesthood does must be done under the direction of those holding the keys or right of presidency.

We Will Teach Our Progenitors

Of necessity the gospel must be both taught and learned by the spirit of revelation, for "if it be by some other way it is not of God" (D&C 50:17–20). The revelations also state that the truth of all things is to be established in the mouth of two or more witnesses (see D&C 6:28), and that missionaries are to go out "two by two" (D&C 42:6). The order of the kingdom in this life is that the primary responsibility for the teaching of the gospel belongs with the family. This complies perfectly with the law of witnesses. Children ought to have the opportunity to hear the gospel taught by a faithful father and the same principles taught again by a faithful mother. They also ought to see the application of those principles in the life of their father and repeated again in the life of their mother. This would be the perfect illustration of the law of witnesses, a mother and father who teach correct principles and a mother and father who set the proper example. These principles do not vary in the world of the spirits. As the primary responsibility for the teaching of the gospel rests with the family here, so it rests with the family there, the difference being that in the world of the spirits there is a greatly extended family. In large measure it will be the responsibility of husband and wife to search out their own progenitors and teach them the gospel. As the primary responsibility for ordinance work rests with the family here, so it will be with the teaching of the gospel there.[5]

The Sisters Will Teach the Sisters

As the institution of the Church aids the family in the teaching of the gospel here, so it will in the world of spirits. As missions are organized here, so they will be there; as we hold group meetings and conferences here, so they will be held in the world of the spirits. Illustrating this principle, President Joseph F. Smith asked: "Who is going to preach the gospel to the women? Who is going to carry the testimony of Jesus Christ to the hearts of the women who have passed away without a knowledge of the gospel?" In response he said it was a simple and obvious thing: women of faith and testimony here who had developed the ability to teach their fellow sisters would be called upon to do so there. Things here are typical of things there, he taught.[6]

All Must Accept the Prophets of Their Own Dispensation

To obtain salvation in this life men must accept the prophets the Lord has called and commissioned to declare the gospel to their own generation. There is no salvation for a man living today who rejects the testimony of Joseph Smith while professing loyalty to Peter, James, and John. No one can profess faith in Joseph Smith and reject the living President of the Church or the other officers and leaders the Lord has chosen to represent him. So it is in the world of the spirits. Those who have lived in our day and died without hearing the gospel will not be taught by Peter or Paul or by Moses or Abraham. They too must accept the gospel at the hands of those commissioned to teach it to their age and generation. Melvin J. Ballard stated the principle thus: "This generation shall receive the Gospel at the hands of those who have been honored with the priesthood of this dispensation. Living or dead, they shall not hear it from anyone else."[7]

Teaching Those of Our Own Nation and Tongue

The heavens have decreed that "every man shall hear the fulness of the gospel in his own tongue, and in his own language, through those who are ordained unto this power" (D&C 90:11). We have every reason to suppose that such decrees transcend the veil of death. Those in that world will also be taught by those of their same nation and tongue. A manifestation given to Oscar W. McConkie while he was serving as president of the California Mission sustains such a conclusion.

A Cochapa Indian by the name of Mark Johnson Vest was baptized in President McConkie's mission, which at that time included parts of Arizona. Mark Vest was a giant of a man with a spirit to match. He stood six feet five inches tall and weighed over three hundred pounds. By birth he would have been the chief of his tribe had his people been following the traditions of their fathers. After he had been in the Church a short time he was called to be the branch president over a small Indian branch. Within six months he had increased the branch to seventy-five members. Brother Vest became ill and in the course of his illness lost over a hundred pounds. Both President McConkie and Elder Harold B. Lee administered to him but without lasting effect. Despite his illness, Mark Vest continued in his work with his people until his death a short time later.

When President McConkie received word that Mark had died he immediately boarded a train for Arizona to attend the funeral. All night long as he traveled, he prayed to know why the Lord had allowed this great missionary to be taken. As he prayed, a vision was opened to him of the spirit world. He saw Mark Johnson Vest standing in front of a large group of Lamanites, which he estimated to be twenty to thirty thousand. As he did so, one of the Indians in the middle of the group stood up and said: "Do not listen to this man! He is not a Lamanite. He is a Nephite!" President McConkie saw Mark Vest rise to the full stature of his height and say: "I am not a Nephite! I am a Lamanite, and when I died I was cremated according to the custom of my people." At this point the vision closed up.

Upon his arrival in Mesa, and as he drove to the chapel where the funeral was to be held, President McConkie was advised of a conflict between Mark Vest's tribe and the tribe from which his wife came. Mark's family wanted him buried in a cemetery while his wife's people wanted to cremate his body according to their traditions. The matter had become so heated that Mark's wife's tribe had threatened to dig up his body and take it if their demands were not met. When they arrived at the chapel President McConkie learned that he was to be the speaker. In his sermon, he was able to resolve the difficulty, explaining the importance of Mark complying even in death with the customs of those among whom he had now been called to labor.

Conclusion

Peter's simple statement that those in the spirit world are to "be judged according to men in the flesh" speaks volumes. If judgment is the same and, as we have learned from the Vision of the Redemption of the Dead, the gospel is the same; and if the source of the gospel is the same, that is, revelation; and if the authority by which it is preached is the same; and if all men are to be taught by the prophets and missionaries of their own dispensation; and if we know that the nature or disposition of men does not change—would we not reason that the degree of ease or difficulty associated with accepting the gospel will be the same also? Surely the justice of God demands it! We could not suppose that those who did not have the opportunity to hear the gospel in this life—who would have accepted it had that chance come to them—will find themselves in a situation that would make it infinitely more difficult in the spirit world. Nor could justice be found in a system demanding of some that they accept the gospel on earth in the most trying of circumstances— being called upon to lay their all upon the altar—while others of their brothers and sisters, having no such challenges in mortality, are granted the gospel in the spirit world in some sort of a blissful paradise where the veil has been lifted and they walk by sight, having no need for faith.

Scripture and reason bring us to the same conclusion— if God is no respecter of persons, then all will be called upon to accept or reject the gospel and work out their salvation in circumstances that the wisdom of heaven holds as equal. None of Adam's family were to be born in the Garden of Eden in a paradisiacal state. All that know accountability were also to know life in the lone and dreary world. All such were to be tried and tested—if not here, then hereafter—all are agents unto themselves and must make a choice for the kingdom of God or against it, and all are to be judged according to men in the flesh—for there is but one gospel, one plan of salvation, one path that leads to eternal life, and one standard of judgment.

5

Spirits: Their Knowledge and Power

If a person gains more knowledge and intelligence in this life through his diligence and obedience than another, he will have so much the advantage in the world to come.
—D&C 130:19

Does death bring a restoration of pre-earth knowledge as many Latter-day Saints have supposed? Is there a need for faith in the spirit world? What are the desires and interests of spirits? Could a spirit apostatize from his station in paradise? Do spirits hear the gospel as soon as they arrive in the world of the spirits or are there great periods of waiting? Would all spirits tell us the same thing were we to communicate with them? What help could spirits give were they allowed to return? Do spirits learn more quickly than mortals or do they learn with greater difficulty? What is it that gives spirits a compelling interest in those of us in mortality? Let us turn to scriptures and prophets in answering such questions.

Death: Reward or Punishment?

Death Is a Judgment

In death the body and spirit are separated for a time; the body is consigned to an earthly grave and returns for a season to the dust from which it was made. The grave lays claim to all that is mortal—every honor, power, glory, or wealth that earth bestows, earth reclaims. Life's blessings and cursings are no more. Disease, bodily pain, poverty, and hunger are but memories. And what of the spirit? What can it take with it in its journey to the world of spirits, in which it will await the resurrection and the great day of judgment? "And I heard a voice from heaven saying unto me, Write, Blessed are the dead which die in the Lord from henceforth: Yea, saith the Spirit, that they may rest from their labours; and their works do follow them" (Revelation 14:13). "And it shall come to pass that those that die in me shall not taste of death, for it shall be sweet unto them" (D&C 42:46). "And then shall it come to pass, that the spirits of those who are righteous are received into a state of happiness, which is called paradise, a state of rest, a state of peace, where they shall rest from all their troubles and from all care, and sorrow" (Alma 40:12). The spirits of the wicked, however, will reap as they have sown, for "they chose evil works rather than good" (Alma 40:13), and such are the works that will follow them.

It cannot be stated more plainly. It will be the seeds of obedience planted and nurtured in the soil of mortality that produce the delicious fruits upon which one feasts in the paradise of God. "It is not the grace of God standing alone; it is not confessing the Lord Jesus with our lips and stopping there; it is not mere belief; it is not church membership as such; it is not a position of prominence or dignity in the Church; it is not any one or all of the thousand winds of doctrine that blow through the sectarian world. It is plain, simple obedience to the laws and ordinances of the gospel."[1] Death, which must come to all men, brings with it an inheritance in paradise or the consignment to hell. It is a judgment. "And unto every kingdom is given a law; and unto every law there are certain bounds also and conditions. All beings who abide not in those conditions are not justified [that is, they cannot inherit that kingdom, they cannot enjoy that glory]. For intelligence [which is 'light and truth'

(D&C 93:36)] cleaveth unto intelligence; wisdom receiveth wisdom; truth embraceth truth; virtue loveth virtue; light cleaveth unto light; mercy hath compassion on mercy and claimeth her own; justice continueth its course and claimeth its own; judgment goeth before the face of him who sitteth upon the throne and governeth and executeth all things." (D&C 88:38–40.) Yes, death is a judgment, for those who sought light will be united with children of light; those who knew nought but darkness will inherit the same. "Thus did I, the Lord God, appoint unto man the days of his probation —that by his natural death he might be raised in immortality unto eternal life, even as many as would believe; and they that believe not unto eternal damnation; for they cannot be redeemed from their spiritual fall, because they repent not; for they love darkness rather than light, and their deeds are evil, and they receive their wages of whom they list to obey" (D&C 29:43–45). Truly our works follow us.

There Is No Apostasy from Paradise

The time of testing and trial is not without its limits and bounds; the day of probation must end. The pre-earth life was a time of schooling, of trials, and of tests. Its inhabitants had agency, and were required to "choose good or evil." Those choosing good found it necessary to exercise "exceedingly great faith" to survive the challenges of that existence. (Alma 13:3–4.) It was a probationary estate, one in which "a third part of the hosts of heaven" were cast out and became perdition, or hopelessly lost. These will not be born into mortality, will never clothe their spirits in bodies, will never obtain any degree of glory.

Those who kept their first estate will be born into mortality, where trials and tests will continue. Of their number, those who have the privilege of accepting the gospel, and who do so—honoring their covenants and enduring in faith—will at death be escorted into the paradise of God, the day of their probation being complete. None such can fall, none such can lose the sure promises of eternal life which are now theirs, the day of their probation being past. They departed "mortal life, firm in the hope of a glorious resurrection, through the grace of God the Father and his Only Begotten Son, Jesus Christ" (D&C 138:14). Abraham taught these principles in this language: "And they who keep their first estate shall be added upon; and they who keep not their first estate shall not have glory in the same kingdom with those who keep their first estate; and they who keep their second estate shall have glory added upon their heads for ever and ever" (Abraham 3:26).

The Knowledge and Power of Those in Paradise

No Restoration of Pre-earth Knowledge

There are those who suppose that death brings with it a restoration of pre-earth knowledge. The scriptures do not sustain such an idea. Were this the case, those in the spirit world who had not heard the gospel could hardly be judged according to men in the flesh, as revelation ancient and modern asserts (see 1 Peter 4:6; D&C 138:10). Such faith would be supplanted by knowledge. Yet, without faith it is impossible to please God (see Heb. 11:6). The fruits of the tree of knowledge must be plucked individually; they do not just fall into our baskets. "For behold, thus saith the Lord God: I will give unto the children of men line upon line, precept upon precept, here a little and there a little; and blessed are those who hearken unto my precepts, and lend an ear unto my counsel, for they shall learn wisdom; for unto him that receiveth I will give more; and from them that shall say, We have enough, from them shall be taken away even that which they have" (2 Nephi 28:30).

God does not give us that for which we are not prepared. None have taught the principle more plainly than Alma, who said, "It is given unto many to know the mysteries of God; nevertheless they are laid under a strict command that they shall not impart only according to the portion of his word which he doth grant unto the children of men, according to the heed and diligence which they give unto him." We have every reason to suppose that this principle is as operative in the spirit world as it is in mortality. "And therefore, he that will harden his heart, the same receiveth the lesser portion of the word; and he that will not harden his heart, to him is given the greater portion of the word, until it is given unto him to know the mysteries of God until he know them in full." Surely that God who would not cast "pearls before swine" in this life will not do so in the world to come. "And they that will harden their hearts," Alma concluded, "to them is given the lesser portion of the word until they know nothing concerning his mysteries; and then they are taken captive by the devil, and led by his will down to destruction. *Now this is what is meant by the chains of hell.*" (Alma 12:9–11; italics added.) By definition, *hell* is to be without the light of the gospel.

It is the faithful who have been promised that they will receive "line upon line, precept upon precept" until they in "due time" receive a fulness of the Father (D&C 98:12; 93:19). The promise is to none else: they who receive the light, and continue in that light, "receiveth more light: and that light groweth brighter and brighter until the perfect day" (D&C 50:24).

Service Brings Salvation

Among the marvelous revelations restored to our dispensation is a fragment of a Gospel apparently written by John the Baptist. From John's writing we learn that Christ did not obtain a fulness of the glory of the Father at first, but did so by advancing from grace to grace. We are then told that this knowledge has been restored to us that we might know *what* and *how* to worship. (See D&C 93:11–19.) That is, we worship by imitating or emulating Christ, who was fully obedient to the will of his Father and who refined his soul, advancing from one grace to a greater grace through service to his fellow beings. Nothing is more exalting to the soul than selfless service. The genius of the Lord's kingdom is that all are called upon to serve—and the more faithful the service, the more godlike the servant becomes. Again, such is the system on earth and such is the system in the world of spirits where "just men" are "made perfect."

As to that world, we do not speak of such things as harps, and clouds, and angels with wings. We speak of servants of God, each faithfully laboring according to assignment, each standing in his own office, laboring in his own calling. Though the paradise of God is a place of rest from the cares and sorrows of life, it is not a place of idleness; it is the spirit's Sabbath, a time and season free from the mundane in which full attention can be given to the things of most worth. Wilford Woodruff illustrated that idea thus:

> Joseph Smith continued visiting myself and others up to a certain time, and then it stopped. The last time I saw him was in heaven. In the night vision I saw him at the door of the temple in heaven. He came to me and spoke to me. He said he could not stop to talk with me because he was in a hurry. The next man I met was Father Smith; he could not talk with me because he was in a hurry. I met half a dozen brethren who had held high positions on earth, and none of them could stop to talk with me because they were in a hurry. I was much astonished. By and by I saw the Prophet again and I got the privilege of asking him a question.
>
> "Now," said I, "I want to know why you are in a hurry. I have been in a hurry all my life; but I expected my hurry would be over when I got into the kingdom of heaven, if I ever did."
>
> Joseph said: "I will tell you, Brother Woodruff. Every dispensation that has had the priesthood on the earth and has gone into the celestial kingdom has had a certain amount of work to do to prepare to go to the earth with the Savior when he goes to reign on the earth. Each dispensation has had ample time to do this work. We have not. We are the last dispensation, and so much work has to be done, and we need to be in a hurry in order to accomplish it." Of course, that was satisfactory, but it was new doctrine to me.[2]

How perfect the system! In the spirit world all faithful Saints are called to the full-time service of the Lord, all assume positions of responsibility and leadership, and all receive the blessings attending such service. Our departed dead but serve in another field of labor, one in which their talents and their opportunities to build up the kingdom of God and to establish his righteousness are multiplied a hundredfold.

Where Darkness Reigns

When Spirits Hear the Gospel

Do all the people who die without the gospel have the opportunity to receive it as soon as they arrive in the spirit world? If we reason from what we know of things in this world, the answer to our question is no. God has offered the gospel with its priesthood, powers, and blessings at various times to the peoples of the earth only to have it rejected. The consequence has been that generations of men have lived and died in ignorance of its principles. Surely there have been but few of earth's inhabitants who have actively sought after the saving truths of the gospel. Men, it appears, prefer religions of their own making and governments and laws of their own design.

"I have not the least doubt but there are spirits there who have dwelt there a thousand years," ventured Parley P. Pratt, "who, if we could converse with them face to face, would be found as ignorant of the truths, the ordinances, powers, keys, Priesthood, resurrection, eternal life of the body, in short, as ignorant of the fulness of the Gospel, with its hopes and consolations," as the religious and political leaders of our day. And why such ignorance among departed spirits? "Because a portion of the inhabitants there are found unworthy of the consolations of the Gospel, until the fulness of time, until they have suffered in hell, in the dungeons of darkness, or the prisons of the condemned, amid the buffetings of fiends, and malicious and lying spirits."[3]

How long must such spirits wait? "You may reckon for yourselves," Elder Pratt said. "The long ages, centuries, thousands of years which intervened between the flood of Noah and the death of Christ. Oh! the weariness, the tardy movement of time, the lingering ages for a people to dwell in condemnation, darkness, ignorance, and despondency, as a punishment for their sins. For they had been filled with violence while on the earth in the flesh, and had rejected the preaching of Noah, and the Prophets which were before him."[4]

From Noah to Christ, some twenty-four hundred years, those destroyed in the flood were left to linger without hope, without exposure to the gospel message in the spirit world. A similar period has passed from the time of the meridian apostasy to the latter-day restoration, in which the great majority of those in the flesh did not hear the gospel. Thus, on both sides of the veil there have been long nights of darkness, nights without even the hope of a dawn.

Ignorant Spirits Cannot Reveal Truth

You cannot teach what you do not know; it is not for darkness to give instruction to light. Were we to converse with the spirits consigned to hell, spirits who knew not the gospel in this life and are as yet to be taught in the spirit world, the spirits of thieves, adulterers, whoremongers, and liars, they could teach us nothing of saving truths. Indeed, we and our fellow Saints may yet be called to minister among them, and when that day comes we will be sent forth to teach and not to be taught (see D&C 43:15). Even among the more refined of the citizenry of this place commonly called the spirit prison there will be found no enlightenment for the Saints. Parley P. Pratt aptly describes their situation thus:

> Take another class of spirits—pious, well-disposed men; for instance, the honest Quaker, Presbyterian, or other sectarian, who, although honest, and well disposed, had not, while in the flesh, the privilege of the Priesthood and Gospel. They believed in Jesus Christ, but died in ignorance of his ordinances, and had not clear conceptions of his doctrine, and of the resurrection. They expected to go to that place called

heaven, as soon as they were dead, and that their doom would then and there be fixed, without any further alteration or preparation.

Suppose they should come back, with liberty to tell all they know? How much light could we get from them? They could only tell you about the nature of things in the world in which they live. And even that world you could not comprehend, by their description thereof, any more than you can describe colours to a man born blind, or sounds to those who have never heard.

What, then, could you get from them? Why, common chit chat, in which there would be a mixture of truth, and of error and mistakes, in mingled confusion: all their communications would betray the same want of clear and logical conceptions, and sound sense and philosophy, as would characterize the same class of spirits in the flesh.[5]

Who Can Be Ministering Spirits?

Who then among the spirits in the spirit world are able to be ministering spirits? Who can come to guide and advise, to confer consolation, to administer to the sick, carry messages of joy and gladness, or, as necessary, warn and protect? "All that have been raised from the dead, and clothed with immortality, all that have ascended to yonder heavens, and been crowned as Kings and Priests, all such are our fellow servants, and of our brethren the Prophets, who have the testimony of Jesus; all such are waiting for the work of God among their posterity on the earth."[6] Abraham, Isaac, and Jacob are the illustrations, for of them we read, "They have entered into their exaltation, according to the promises, and sit upon thrones, and are not angels but are gods" (D&C 132:37). "Yea, and Enoch also, and they who were with him; the prophets who were before him; and Noah also, and they who were before him; and Moses also, and they who were before him; and from Moses to Elijah, and from Elijah to John, who were with Christ in his resurrection" (D&C 133:54–55).

Who else can serve as ministering servants? Any who departed this world and went thereafter not to that place of sorrow and darkness, but to the paradise of God, to that place of righteousness, peace, light, and truth. These—

persons referred to in scripture as "just men made perfect" (D&C 129:3), as well as translated beings such as John the Revelator, the Three Nephites, or other holy beings of whom we know not (D&C 49:8)—minister to those of us still in the flesh.

The Time Necessary to Learn in the Spirit World

Is it easier or more difficult to learn in the world of the spirits? Again we return to the touchstone given us by Peter —spirits are to be judged according to men in the flesh. If learning were easier and repentance quicker in the spirit world, then there would be little meaning in the declaration of the Lord that "if a person gains more knowledge and intelligence in this life through his diligence and obedience than another, he will have so much the advantage in the world to come" (D&C 130:19). Might we not say that those who have trained their eyes to see and their ears to hear will see and hear with far greater facility, while those who have not done so must then learn to do so with painstaking effort?

Why the Dead Have Such Interest in the Living

What is there about mortality that would be of interest to those in the spirit world? When they look upon this life, where are their eyes turned? We answer: to the Latter-day Saints. And why? Because it is among this people and this people alone that the keys, authority, and ordinances are found by which the dead can be redeemed. We ask, are any other people building holy sanctuaries for the conversations and ministrations pertaining to the salvation of the dead? "No, verily. No other people have opened their hearts to conceive ideas so grand. No other people have their sympathies drawn out to such an extent toward the fathers. . . . It is here that the countless millions of the spirit world would look for the ordinances of redemption, so far as they have been enlightened by the preaching of the Gospel, since the keys of the former dispensations were taken away from the earth."[7]

Conclusion

Four hundred years before the birth of Christ, Malachi, the last of the Old Testament prophets, penned words that would seal the Old Testament with a spirit of faith and hope. His was the promise of the return of Elijah and the sealing powers by which the family chain is linked throughout all the generations of time and throughout all eternity. Truly he promised that the hearts of the fathers, those who have gone on, would turn to their children in the flesh and that there would be a link or bond between the two, each laboring to bless the other. We do not walk alone, for we have righteous fathers who both know and bless us.

6

Angels: Our Companions

*Have angels ceased to appear unto the children of men?
Or has he withheld the power of the Holy Ghost from them? Or
will he, so long as time shall last, or the earth shall stand,
or there shall be one man upon the face thereof to be saved?
Behold I say unto you, Nay; for it is by faith that miracles
are wrought; and it is by faith that angels appear and minister unto men; wherefore, if these things have ceased wo be
unto the children of men, for it is because of unbelief, and all
is vain.*

—Moroni 7:36

There never has been a gospel dispensation without the ministering of angels. A people who cannot claim the ministering of angels cannot claim an everlasting gospel. Without the
ministering of angels we could make no pretense to priesthood, its keys, power, or authority. Without the ministering
of angels we would be without the sealing power by which
families and generations are bound together and by which
all are bound to the heavens. Without the ministering of
angels and other forms of revelation, our theology would be
like a body without a spirit.

Messengers of Salvation

"And thus the Gospel began to be preached, from the beginning, being declared by holy angels sent forth from the presence of God, and by his own voice, and by the gift of the Holy Ghost" (Moses 5:58). Such is Moses' summary of the manner in which the gospel of Christ has been taught from the days of Adam. Moses himself having been "ordained by the hand of angels" (JST Galatians 3:19), and having been instructed by them in the law that he gave Israel (see Acts 7:53), knew whereof he spoke. Similarly, Moroni declared, "For behold, God knowing all things, being from everlasting to everlasting, behold, he sent angels to minister unto the children of men, to make manifest concerning the coming of Christ; and in Christ there should come every good thing" (Moroni 7:22).

From earth's beginning, angels had heralded the day of Christ's birth, as did the angelic host on that Christmas eve to chosen shepherds of Bethlehem (see Luke 2:9–14). For the time of his coming was to be "made known unto just and holy men, by the mouth of angels," the world over (Alma 13:26). Nor were these "glad tidings" and this "joyful news" for prophets and righteous men alone. Alma testified: "He imparteth his word by angels unto men, yea, not only men but women also. Now this is not all; little children do have words given unto them many times, which confound the wise and the learned." (Alma 32:23.)

Nowhere do we see the relationship between angels and mortals more perfectly manifest than in the ministry of the Savior. In a beautiful messianic psalm David wrote: "For he shall give his angels charge over thee, to keep thee in all thy ways. They shall bear thee up in their hands, lest thou dash thy foot against a stone." (Psalm 91:11–12.) Angels were his companions from the preparation for his ministry when they "ministered unto him" (Mark 1:13) to the agony of Gethsemane where the angel strengthened him (see Luke 22:43). Angels tended his empty tomb and testified of his resurrection (see Luke 24:4–5), as legions of men and women came forth from the grave with him and went into the "holy city, and appeared unto many" (Matthew 27:53). In the Americas a similar event took place in fulfillment of the prophecy of Samuel (see Helaman 14:23–25; 3 Nephi 23:9–11). Such was the pattern of Christ's day and such of necessity must be the pattern for our day.

Angels: Who Are They?

Since angels have come from the days of Adam to testify of Christ, teach his gospel, prophesy in his name, and otherwise labor as the Lord's messengers, might we in propriety ask who they are? Are they to be faceless and nameless? Is it a requirement of their ministry that they be strangers to us or is it appropriate that we know them? From whence do they come and what is their nature?

By revelation Joseph Smith learned that "there are no angels who minister to this earth but those who do belong or have belonged to it" (D&C 130:5). Thus, Joseph F. Smith observed that

> when messengers are sent to minister to the inhabitants of this earth, they are not strangers, but from the ranks of our kindred, friends, and fellow-beings and fellow-servants. The ancient prophets who died were those who came to visit their fellow creatures upon the earth. They came to Abraham, to Isaac, and to Jacob; it was such beings—holy beings if you please—who waited upon the Savior and administered to him on the Mount. The angel that visited John, when an exile, and unfolded to his vision future events in the history of man upon the earth, was one who had been here, who had toiled and suffered in common with the people of God; for you remember that John, after his eyes had beheld the glories of the great future, was about to fall down and worship him, but was peremptorily forbidden to do so. "See thou do it not; for I am thy fellow-servant, and of thy brethren the prophets, and of them which keep the sayings of this book. . . ."
>
> In like manner our fathers and mothers, brothers, sisters and friends who have passed away from this earth, having been faithful, and worthy to enjoy these rights and privileges,

may have a mission given them to visit their relatives and friends upon the earth again, bring from the divine Presence messages of love, of warning, or reproof and instruction, to those whom they had learned to love in the flesh. . . .

Joseph Smith, Hyrum Smith, Brigham Young, Heber C. Kimball, Jedediah M. Grant, David Patten, Joseph Smith, Sen., and all those noble men who took an active part in the establishment of this work, and who died true and faithful to their trust, have the right and privilege, and possess the keys and power, to minister to the people of God in the flesh who live now, as much so and on the same principle as the ancient servants of God had the right to return to the earth and minister to the Saints of God in their day.[1]

It seems reasonable to suppose that no previous dispensation will match our dispensation, the dispensation of the fulness of times, in the number or diversity of angelic visitors. First, it is our privilege to have all the keys, powers, and authorities of past dispensations restored to us. Among those who came to the Prophet Joseph Smith for this purpose were Adam or Michael, the archangel; Raphael, who may also be Enoch; Noah, or Gabriel; an Elias from Abraham's dispensation, possibly Melchizedek or maybe Abraham himself; Moses; Elijah; John the Baptist; and Peter, James, and John. Each of these came to bring the powers and authority peculiar to his own office and calling and the dispensation of which he was a part. From among the Book of Mormon peoples we have record that Joseph Smith was visited by Nephi, Mormon, the Three Nephites, and of course on many occasions by Moroni. We are told that many other angels came, and we understand their number to have included such notables as Seth, Jacob, and Paul.[2] In all such visits it was the established pattern for the angelic visitor to introduce himself by name and to identify the authority that was his.

The appearance of angelic ministrants was so common to this period of the Church's history that the Prophet saw fit to include a revelation in the Doctrine and Covenants giving the manner in which counterfeit angels are detected.

The revelation notes that messengers of God might be either resurrected beings or "just men made perfect," that is, messengers from the spirit world who will be numbered among the glorified in the day of their resurrection. Therefore, we are instructed that when a messenger comes saying he has a message from God, we are to offer him our hand and request him to shake hands. If he is a resurrected being he will do so and we will feel his hand. If he is a just man made perfect, he will not shake hands with us but will remain and deliver his message. "If he be the devil as an angel of light, when you ask him to shake hands he will offer you his hand, and you will not feel anything; you may therefore detect him." (D&C 129.)

More frequently, angelic labors will go undetected. Included in this category would be the labors of translated beings—John the Revelator, who labors to gather the tribes of Israel (see D&C 77:14); the three Nephites, who labor with both Jew and Gentile and will not be known by them (see 3 Nephi 28:7, 27–28); along with other "holy men" that we "know not of" (see D&C 49:8; Matthew 16:28; Mark 9:1; Luke 9:27). We will yet speak of the interest of our departed family members and Church leaders as manifest by their attendance at such things as temple dedications, special conferences, and so forth, along with their unseen though often felt presence on special occasions within the family.

By What Authority Angels Come

Order is a hallmark of the kingdom of God here and hereafter. Paradise is not a place of confusion or disarray. It is a kingdom of laws and government, a kingdom in which all of its citizens zealously labor in their own office and in their own calling. Promiscuous or indiscriminate meddling in the affairs of mortals is not a prerogative known to its inhabitants, nor is it one that they would attempt to usurp. The populace of such a kingdom would not respond to the enticements of mediums or spiritualists. Nothing could be more inconsistent than to suppose that prophets of God or other righteous holders of the priesthood would be at the beck and call of these soothsayers. It is inconceivable that men like Isaiah, Jeremiah, Peter, James, John, Paul, Joseph Smith, or Brigham Young, would respond to the call of false prophets or prophetesses.

It will be remembered that Saul, who was rejected of the Lord because of his disobedience, and who could no longer receive revelation from God, improperly sought the aid of the witch of En-dor for that purpose. At the king's request she conjured up a spirit purporting to be the prophet Samuel. This evil spirit rightly prophesied Saul's death and that of his sons in the battle of the next day. (See 1 Samuel 28.) From corrections in Joseph Smith's translation of this text we learn that Saul did not actually see Samuel but rather relied upon what the witch said she was seeing. In any event we know that Samuel, who was then in the paradise of God, would not respond to the biddings of this evil woman in death any more than he would have in life.

The manner in which the government of God continues beyond the veil is evident in Joseph Smith's description of the restoration of the Aaronic Priesthood. "The messenger who visited us on this occasion and conferred this Priesthood upon us," Joseph wrote, "said that his name was John, the same that is called John the Baptist in the New Testament, and that he acted under the direction of Peter, James, and John, who held the keys of the Priesthood of Melchizedek" (Joseph Smith—History 1:72). The following facts can be identified from this brief excerpt: (1) John's introduction of himself by name and association with the New Testament; (2) his identification of the authority that he held in mortality and took with him to the spirit world; (3) the announcement that he was going to bestow that authority upon Joseph and Oliver Cowdery; (4) the reference to the position of presidency held by Peter, James, and John, which authority they too had taken with them beyond the veil; (5) and that he acted under the direction of Peter, James, and John, honoring their position of presidency in the realms of glory as he honored that same authority in mortality. Poignantly, John referred to Joseph and Oliver, as his "fellow servants" (Joseph Smith—History 1:69), thus linking them with himself as a part of the same great brotherhood of priesthood and as chosen servants of the same God.

Our example illustrates that when God has something to reveal by the ministering of angels, it will come in the way, by the means, and through the person or persons whom he has appointed. Nor can it be without significance that among those keys, or that presidency, restored by the Baptist were *"the keys of the ministering of angels."* Thus, as the foundations of authority are laid in our dispensation, we have given to us the means by which we can call upon the power of those beyond the veil for protection, guidance, comfort, and strength.[3] The ministry of angels takes many forms, as the ministry of the priesthood takes many forms in mortality. As with all messengers of the Lord their primary responsibility is that of revealers and teachers of the truths of salvation. Nephi tells us that "angels speak by the power of the Holy Ghost; wherefore, they speak the words of Christ" (2 Nephi 32:3). Thus we share with our "fellow servants" on the other side of the veil, and with those who labor here as translated beings, the same gospel, the same priesthood, the same responsibility to act under the direction of the keys of the priesthood, and the same right to the Holy Ghost by which we are to teach, preach, and bless others.

Between us and those in the spirit world a veil has been wisely drawn, yet it is not impenetrable. "As the living are not in their mortal condition, able to see and converse with the dead, so it is rational to believe, the inhabitants of the spiritual domain are, in their normal condition, shut out from intercourse with men in the flesh. By permission of the Lord, persons on either side of the veil may be manifest to those on the other, but this will certainly be by law and according to the order which God has established."[4]

Some of the Purposes for Which Angels Come

The key requisites for such an experience are obviously worthiness and appropriate purpose. Illustrating this, Wilford

Woodruff recalled that a member of the Quorum of the Twelve told him that he had prayed for many years to enjoy the administration of an angel but that his prayers had never been answered. "I said to him that if he were to pray a thousand years to the God of Israel for that gift, it would not be granted, unless the Lord had a motive in sending an angel to him. I told him that the Lord never did nor never will send an angel to anybody merely to gratify the desire of the individual to see an angel. If the Lord sends an angel to anyone, He sends him to perform a work that cannot be performed [except] by the administration of an angel."[5]

Instruction and Prophecy

As messengers of the Lord, the primary purpose for which angels minister among men is to teach and testify of the saving principles of the gospel. "The office of their ministry," Moroni taught us, "is to call men unto repentance, and to fulfil and to do the work of the covenants of the Father . . . by declaring the word of Christ unto the chosen vessels of the Lord, that they might bear testimony of him" (Moroni 7:31). Their very purpose constitutes a standard by which delusive spirits can be discerned, for "that which doth not edify is not of God" (D&C 50:23), whereas to edify is to enlighten through teaching and instruction. Thus, the angels of the Lord are primarily gospel teachers, the pattern of their discourses being a perfect example after which we ought to pattern our own.

Illustrations of the manner in which angels have instructed the children of the Lord are legion. Nephi had an angel as his tutor as he saw the vision of the birth of Christ. In that instruction the angel inquired as to Nephi's understanding and then revealed to him marvelous truths that Nephi in turn recorded for us. (See 1 Nephi 11–14.) Similarly, Joseph Smith spoke of "conversing" with Moroni and of his "interviews" in which he received "instructions and intelligence" (Joseph Smith—History 1:42, 47, 54). John the Revelator's experience in receiving what we know as the book of Revelation appears to have been one and the same with that of Nephi (see Revelation 1, 19). Nephi's younger brother, Jacob, was also taught much about the destiny of Israel and the coming of Christ by an angel (see 2 Nephi 10:3). King Benjamin delivered to his people a great discourse replete with messianic prophecy, which he also had received at the hands of an angel (see Mosiah 3).

The experiences recorded in the scriptures establish the principle. They are not intended to limit the ministering of angels to prophets any more than the recording of the prophets' revelations are intended to limit the receipt of revelation to prophets. To those who have received the Melchizedek Priesthood and honor the covenants thus made, the Lord said, "I have given the heavenly hosts and mine angels charge concerning you" (D&C 84:42). In the dedicatory prayer of the Kirtland Temple, Joseph Smith prayed that those there endowed might "go forth from this house armed with thy power," in the name of the Lord, that his "glory be round about them" and his "angels have charge over them" (D&C 109:22).

There are, as we have noted, proper limitations to the ministering of angels, but these bounds are not associated with offices and callings. Illustrating this principle with his missionary experiences, Wilford Woodruff said, "I went out as a priest, and my companion as an elder, and we traveled thousands of miles, and had many things manifested to us. I desire to impress upon you the fact that it does not make any difference whether a man is a priest or an apostle, if he magnifies his calling. A priest holds the key of the ministering of angels. Never in my life, as an apostle, as a seventy, or as an elder, have I ever had more of the protection of the Lord than while holding the office [of] a priest. The Lord revealed to me by visions, by revelations, and by the Holy Spirit, many things that lay before me."[6]

Warning and Protecting

The scriptures amply attest that armies or legions of angels have been marshaled on the other side of the veil to protect the Saints of God in mortality. One of the early illustrations of this in the scriptures is Joshua's experience after he and the army of Israel had crossed the Jordan. It was near Jericho that Joshua saw a man with his sword drawn, and said to him, "Art thou for us, or for our adversaries? And he said, Nay; but as captain of the host of the Lord am I now come. And Joshua fell on his face to the earth, and did worship, and said unto him, What saith my lord unto his servant? And the captain of the Lord's host said unto Joshua, Loose thy shoe from off thy foot; for the place whereon thou standest is holy. And Joshua did so." (Joshua 5:13–15.)

Another classic illustration took place when an army from Syria surrounded the city of Dothan to take Elisha prisoner. Having arisen early, one of Elisha's young disciples discovered the trap that had been laid for the prophet and manifest great fear. Unperturbed, Elisha responded: "Fear not: for they that be with us are more than they that be with them. And Elisha prayed, and said, Lord, I pray thee, open his eyes, that he may see. And the Lord opened the eyes of the young man; and he saw: and, behold, the mountain was full of horses and chariots of fire round about Elisha. And when they came down to him, Elisha prayed unto the Lord, and said, Smite this people, I pray thee, with blindness. And he smote them with blindness according to the word of Elisha." (2 Kgs. 6:16–18.)

It will also be remembered that Nephi and Sam were spared a beating by Laman and Lemuel through the intervention of an angel of the Lord (see 1 Nephi 3:29); that Daniel had an angel as his companion when he was thrown into the lions' den (see Daniel 6:22); that Shadrach, Meshach, and Abed-nego also enjoyed the company of an angel when they were cast into the fiery furnace (see Daniel 3:25); that Helaman's sons, the prophets Nephi and Lehi, were protected by fire from those who sought to kill them, "and angels came down out of heaven and ministered unto them," before some three hundred witnesses (Helaman 5:21–49).

As to our own dispensation, it will be remembered that a heavenly messenger came to Joseph Smith when he set out to procure wine for a sacrament meeting. Joseph was commanded not to purchase wine from his enemies, the intimation being that it was or at some time might be poisoned. It was in this revelation that we learned that it did not matter what we eat or drink in the ordinances of the sacrament, if it was performed in the proper spirit. (See D&C 27:1–4). On another occasion, Joseph Smith saw Brigham Young in a vision "standing in a strange land, in the far south and west, in a desert place, upon a rock in the midst of about a dozen men of color, who appeared hostile. He was preaching to them in their own tongue, and the angel of God standing above his head, with a drawn sword in his hand, protecting him." Commenting, Joseph said, "But he did not see it."[7]

Blessing, Sustaining, and Comforting

Wilford Woodruff records the following experience which took place in London in October of 1840.

> Having retired to rest in good season, I fell asleep and slept until midnight, when I awoke and meditated upon the things of God until 3 o'clock in the morning; and, while forming a determination to warn the people in London and by the assistance and inspiration of God to overcome the power of darkness, a person appeared to me, whom I consider was the prince of darkness. He made war upon me, and attempted to take my life. As he was about to overcome me I prayed to the Father, in the name of Jesus Christ, for help. I then had power over him and he left me, though I was much wounded. Afterwards three persons dressed in white came to me and prayed with me, and I was healed immediately of all my wounds, and delivered of all my troubles.[8]

In the April 1973 general conference of the Church, Harold B. Lee shared a somewhat similar experience:

> May I impose upon you for a moment to express appreciation for something that happened to me some time ago, years ago. I was suffering from an ulcer condition that was becoming worse and worse. We had been touring a mission; my wife, Joan, and I were impressed the next morning that we

should get home as quickly as possible, although we had planned to stay for some other meetings.

On the way across the country, we were sitting in the forward section of the airplane. Some of our Church members were in the next section. As we approached a certain point en route, someone laid his hand upon my head. I looked up; I could see no one. That happened again before we arrived home, again with the same experience. Who it was, by what means or what medium, I may never know, except I knew that I was receiving a blessing that I came a few hours later to know I needed most desperately.

As soon as we arrived home, my wife very anxiously called the doctor. It was now about 11 o'clock at night. He called me to come to the telephone, and he asked me how I was; and I said, "Well, I am very tired. I think I will be all right." But shortly thereafter, there came massive hemorrhages which, had they occurred while we were in flight, I wouldn't be here today talking about it.[9]

It was also in a conference address that President Joseph F. Smith shared the following impressions about the nature of spirits and their concerns with events on this side of the veil:

> I feel sure that the Prophet Joseph Smith and his associates, who, under the guidance and inspiration of the Almighty, and by his power, began this latter-day work, would rejoice and do rejoice—I was going to say if they were permitted to look down upon the scene that I behold in this tabernacle, but I believe they do have the privilege of looking down upon us just as the all-seeing eye of God beholds every part of His handiwork. For I believe that those who have been chosen in this dispensation and in former dispensations, to lay the foundation of God's work in the midst of the children of men, for their salvation and exaltation, will not be deprived in the spirit world from looking down upon the results of their own labors, efforts and mission assigned them by the wisdom and purpose of God, to help to redeem and to reclaim the children of the Father from their sins.
>
> So I feel quite confident that the eye of Joseph, the Prophet, and of the martyrs of this dispensation, and of

Brigham and John and Wilford, and those faithful men who were associated with them in their ministry upon the earth, are carefully guarding the interests of the Kingdom of God in which they labored and for which they strove during their mortal lives. I believe they are as deeply interested in our welfare today, if not with greater capacity, with far more interest behind the veil, than they were in the flesh. I believe they know more: I believe their minds have expanded beyond their comprehension in mortal life, and their interests are enlarged and expanded in the work of the Lord to which they gave their lives and their best service. . . . I stand in the presence not only of the Father and of the Son, but in the presence of those whom God commissioned, raised up and inspired to lay the foundations of the work in which we are engaged. Accompanying that feeling, I am impressed with the thought that I would not this moment say or do one thing that would be taken as unwise or imprudent, or that would give offense to any of my former associates and co-laborers in the work of the Lord.

I would not like to say one thing or express a thought that would grieve the heart of Joseph, or of Brigham, or of John, or of Wilford, or Lorenzo, or any of their faithful associates in the ministry. Sometimes the Lord expands our vision from this point of view and this side of the veil, that we feel and seem to realize that we can look beyond the thin veil which separates us from that other sphere. If we can see by the enlightening influence of the Spirit of God and through the words that have been spoken by the holy prophets of God, beyond the veil that separates us from the spirit world, surely those who have passed beyond, can see more clearly through the veil back here to us than it is possible for us to see to them from our sphere of action. I believe we move and have our being in the presence of heavenly messengers and of heavenly beings. We are not separate from them. We begin to realize more and more fully, as we become acquainted with the principles of the Gospel, as they have been revealed anew in this dispensation, that we are closely related to our kindred, to our ancestors, to our friends and associates and co-laborers who have preceded us into the spirit world. We can not forget them; we do not cease to love them; we always hold them in our hearts, in memory, and thus we are associated and united to them by ties that we cannot break, and we can not dissolve or free ourselves from.

If this is the case with us in our finite condition, surrounded by our mortal weaknesses, short-sightedness, lack of inspiration and wisdom from time to time, how much more certain it is and reasonable and consistent to believe that those who have been faithful who have gone beyond and are still engaged in the work for the salvation of the souls of men, the opening of the prison doors to them that are bound and proclaiming liberty to the captives who can see us better than we can see them; that they know us better than we know them. They have advanced; we are advancing; we are growing as they have grown; we are reaching the goal that they have attained unto; and therefore, I claim that we live in their presence, they see us, they are solicitous for our welfare, they love us now more than ever. For now they see the dangers that beset us; they can comprehend better than ever before, the weaknesses that are liable to mislead us into dark and forbidden paths. They see the temptations and the evils that beset us in life and the proneness of mortal beings to yield to temptation and to wrong doing; hence their solicitude for us and their love for us and their desire for our well being must be greater than that which we feel for ourselves.

I thank God for the feeling that I possess and enjoy and for the realization that I have, that I stand, not only in the presence of Almighty God, my Maker and Father, but in the presence of His Only Begotten Son in the flesh, the Savior of the world; and I stand in the presence of Peter and James, (and perhaps the eyes of John are also upon us and we know it not); and that I stand also in the presence of Joseph and Hyrum and Brigham and John, and those who have been valiant in the testimony of Jesus Christ and faithful to their mission in the world, who have gone before.[10]

Bringing the Honest in Heart to the Church

Angels often function as missionaries, a classic scriptural illustration being the angel who visited Cornelius. A devout man, Cornelius feared God, gave freely to the poor, and prayed regularly. "Thy prayers and thine alms" the angel said to him, "are come up for a memorial before God" (that is, "Thy good works have opened the windows of heaven to you"). Cornelius was then directed to send for Peter, who would teach him and his household the gospel and baptize them for the remission of their sins. (Acts 10.)

In this same context, Melvin J. Ballard asked the question, "Why is it that sometimes only one of a city or household receives the Gospel?" In response to his question he then shared his revealed insight, "It was made known to me that it is because the righteous dead who have received the Gospel in the spirit world are exercising themselves, and in answer to their prayers elders of the Church are sent to the homes of their posterity so that the Gospel might be taught to them, and that descendant is then privileged to do the work for his dead kindred." He also added, "it is with greater intensity that the hearts of the fathers and mothers in the spirit world are turned to their children now in the flesh than that our hearts are turned to them."[11]

The Presence of the Unseen

Elder Bruce R. McConkie spoke at the funeral of President Joseph Fielding Smith. Later, in a talk at the Joseph F. Smith family reunion, Elder McConkie told that group that Joseph F. Smith had attended the funeral of his son, doing so to manifest his interest in the family. Such interest and concern is most natural. When a righteous man or a righteous woman dies, they do not cease to love their family in the flesh, they do not cease to pray for them, they do not cease to labor in their behalf. As their family was their primary concern in this life, so it will continue to be their primary concern on the other side of the veil. We would demean the nature of their labors in the spirit world to suppose that they had nothing more to do than to conduct a daily watch over those they left behind; yet the love and interest is still there, and on special occasions their presence will be felt and in some instances, as appropriate, they may be granted the privilege to more fully manifest themselves, though these treasures of heaven will not be common.

As the inspiration of heaven most commonly comes while we are on the Lord's errand, such is also the setting in which the intervention of heaven is most common. As a sequel to the Vision of the Celestial Kingdom, Joseph Smith said: "I saw the Twelve Apostles of the Lamb, who are now upon the earth, who hold the keys of this last ministry, in foreign lands, standing together in a circle, much fatigued, with their clothes tattered and feet swollen, with their eyes cast downward, and Jesus standing in their midst, and they did not behold Him. The Savior looked upon them and wept."[12]

In an early revelation to Joseph Smith the Lord said: "Mine eyes are upon you. I am in your midst and ye cannot see me." (D&C 38:7.) Again, to those of our dispensation the Lord said, "Verily, verily, I say unto you, as I said unto my disciples, where two or three are gathered together in my name, as touching one thing, behold, there will I be in the midst of them—even so am I in the midst of you" (D&C 6:32). To some of the early missionaries of our dispensation the Lord said, "I myself will go with them and be in their midst; and I am their advocate with the Father, and nothing shall prevail against them" (D&C 32:3). Such are not idle promises. In a general conference of the Church, Harold B. Lee said: "There has been here an overwhelming spiritual endowment, attesting, no doubt, that in all likelihood we are in the presence of personages, seen and unseen, who are in attendance. Who knows but that even our Lord and Master would be near us on such an occasion as this, for we and the world, must never forget that this is his church, and under his almighty direction we are to serve!"[13] At the conclusion of the same conference President Lee said: "I can't leave this conference without saying to you that I have a conviction that the Master hasn't been absent from us on these occasions. This is his church. Where else would he rather be than right here at the headquarters of his church? He isn't an absentee master; he is concerned about us. He wants us to follow where he leads. I know that he is a living reality, as is our Heavenly Father. I know it."[14]

Conclusion

The faithful who have preceded us into the world of spirits have not ceased to love us, to be concerned about us, to pray for us, or to labor in our behalf. For those sealed by the power of the priesthood, death does not dissolve familial ties. Indeed, the increased understanding that comes to one in the paradise of God could but sharpen the desires to continue to minister in behalf of those who have remained on earth. The faithful man or woman whose life was centered in protecting and blessing their family here will find those feelings greatly intensified on the other side of the veil. We are not alone. Surely in the household of faith all have entertained angels unaware. As Moroni testifies, "If these things have ceased [miracles and ministering of angels], then has faith ceased also; and awful is the state of man, for they are as though there had been no redemption made" (Moroni 7:38).

7

Temples: Our Link
with Eternity

*Verily I say unto you, that your anointings, and your wash-
ings, and your baptisms for the dead, and your solemn
assemblies . . . are ordained by the ordinance of my holy
house, which my people are always commanded to build
unto my holy name. . . . For I deign to reveal unto my church
things which have been kept hid from before the foundation
of the world, things that pertain to the dispensation of the fulness of times.*

—D&C 124:39, 41

The Lord's people have always been a temple people, the
temple being the place of divine encounter, of revelation,
and of covenant. Here the ordinances of salvation are performed for both living and dead. Here the family unit is
created—bonded to ancestry and sealed to posterity. In
temples, the past, present, and future are fused, the seen and
the unseen become one. Temples are the link between the
dead and the living, between time and eternity, between
man and God.

The Revelation of Vicarious Work

It was the Vision of the Celestial Kingdom (D&C 137)
which opened the door to the reality that God judges men

by their hearts as well as their works of righteousness. At what point in time Joseph received the specific revelation regarding salvation for the dead is not presently known. Four and one-half years after the Vision of the Celestial Kingdom was received, the Prophet delivered his first public discourse on the subject of baptism for the dead. The date was 15 August 1840, the occasion a funeral address in behalf of Seymour Brunson, a member of the Nauvoo High Council. Simon Baker was in attendance at the funeral and has left us the following account:

> I was present at a discourse that the prophet Joseph delivered on baptism for the dead 15 August 1840. He read the greater part of the 15th chapter of Corinthians and remarked that the Gospel of Jesus Christ brought glad tidings of great joy. . . . He also said the apostle [Paul] was talking to a people who understood baptism for the dead, for it was practiced among them. He went on to say that people could now act for their friends who had departed this life, and that the plan of salvation was calculated to save all who were willing to obey the requirements of the law of God. He went on and made a very beautiful discourse.[1]

One month later, on 14 September 1840, Joseph Smith Sr., passed away. Just before his death, Father Smith requested that someone be baptized for and in behalf of his oldest son, Alvin. Hyrum complied with his father's last wish, and was baptized by proxy in behalf of his older brother.[2]

In a letter to the Twelve dated 19 October 1840, Joseph Smith commented concerning this new doctrine:

> I presume the doctrine of "baptism for the dead" has ere this reached your ears, and may have raised some inquiries in your minds respecting the same. I cannot in this letter give you all the information you may desire on the subject; but aside from knowledge independent of the Bible, I would say that it was certainly practiced by the ancient churches [then cites 1 Corinthians 15:29]. . . .
>
> I first mentioned the doctrine in public when preaching the funeral sermon of Brother Seymour Brunson: and have since then given general instructions in the Church on the

subject. The Saints have the privilege of being baptized for those of their relatives who are dead, [and now note the Prophet's tie of this doctrine to the Vision of the Celestial Kingdom] *whom they believe would have embraced the Gospel, if they had been privileged with hearing it,* and who have received the Gospel in the spirit, through the instrumentality of those who have been commissioned to preach to them while in prison.

Without enlarging on the subject, you will undoubtedly see its consistency and reasonableness; and it presents the Gospel of Christ in probably a more enlarged scale than some have imagined it.[3]

In the latter part of his ministry, this doctrine became a major focus of the Prophet Joseph Smith. Two sections of the Doctrine and Covenants (127, 128) are letters to the Saints containing instructions regarding the practice of baptism for the dead. Joseph would point out the eternal significance of this doctrine by making such statements as these: "The greatest responsibility in this world that God has laid upon us is to seek after our dead,"[4] and "This doctrine was the burden of the scriptures. Those Saints who neglect it in behalf of their deceased relatives, do it at the peril of their own salvation."[5] In one of the espistles referred to above, Joseph wrote (in September of 1842) that "these are principles in relation to the dead and the living that cannot be lightly passed over, as pertaining to our salvation. For their salvation is necessary and essential to our salvation." (D&C 128:15.)

As with the doctrinal restoration in general, the doctrine of salvation for the dead came line upon line, precept upon precept. In process of time the Saints came to know that men should officiate in behalf of men, women in behalf of women; that ordinances other than baptism for the dead—washings, anointings, endowments, and temple marriages—could be performed on behalf of the dead; that it was acceptable to officiate by proxy for those who were not immediate kin; that men and women should search their genealogical records as far back in time as possible, and then

see to it that all familial ties were sealed together through
appropriate temple ordinances; and that through holy and
sacred edifices dedicated to the Lord Jehovah, the Almighty
would "reveal unto [his] church things which have been
kept hid from before the foundation of the world, things
that pertain to the dispensation of the fulness of times" (D&C
124:41).

The Keys of the Priesthood Restored

As Jesus spoke with his disciples at Caesarea Philippi, the
chief Apostle, in response to a query by his Master, declared,
"Thou art the Christ, the Son of the living God." Peter was
commended for his witness and assured that such a testimony was of divine origin. "And I say also unto thee," the
Savior continued, "that thou art Peter, and upon this rock I
will build my church; and the gates of hell shall not prevail
against it. And *I will give unto thee the keys of the kingdom of
heaven: and whatsoever thou shalt bind on earth shall be
bound in heaven: and whatsoever thou shalt loose on earth
shall be loosed in heaven."* (Matthew 16:13–19; italics added.)
Within a week the Lord's promise was fulfilled; Jesus took
with him Peter, James, and John—the chief Apostles and First
Presidency of the meridian Church—to a high mountain to
pray. While in that setting, these four were transfigured—
lifted spiritually to a higher plane—and thus prepared for a
transcendent experience.

Moses and Elijah appeared and bestowed their keys
upon this meridian presidency.[6] As we have stated before,
keys are directing powers, the right of presidency. These
rights and powers would allow the Apostles to govern and
direct the Church in the absence of Jesus Christ, and to
make available to the members all of the blessings of the
everlasting gospel. Peter, James, and John had received the
Melchizedek Priesthood years earlier and had been given
apostolic power and commission at the time of their
appointment to the Twelve. As a result of this experience on
the Mount of Transfiguration, they were granted the right to

bind and seal on earth, with the full confidence that their actions would receive sealing validity in the heavens.

That which took place in the first century of the Christian Church has its parallels in the latter-day Church. The winter and spring of 1836 proved to be an era of both modern pentecost and modern transfiguration. By early April, bearers of the priesthood had been washed and anointed. Sunday, 3 April 1836, one week following the glorious dedicatory services of the temple, the Brethren were again assembled in the house of the Lord. In the morning hours, Elder Thomas B. Marsh (then President of the Twelve) and Elder David W. Patten were called upon to speak. In the afternoon the First Presidency and the Apostles participated in a sacramental service, after which Joseph Smith and Oliver Cowdery knelt in prayer behind drawn curtains adjacent to the large pulpits on the west side of the main floor of the temple. At that moment a wondrous vision burst upon them, one of the most important theophanies of the ages.

The Appearance of the Savior

Just as Jesus and his three ancient Apostles were transfigured in the first century, so also were Joseph and Oliver— "apostles, and especial witnesses" of the name of Christ (D&C 27:12)—transformed and made ready to penetrate the veil and receive divine direction and authority. Appropriately, Jesus the Christ appeared first. In the wanderings of ancient Israel, Jehovah had chosen frequently to make his presence known and manifest his glory through a cloud which rested upon his temple. On this sacred day, Jehovah came again to his temple—the first to be authorized and accepted by him since the long night of apostate darkness. (Cf. Exodus 24:9–10; Revelation 1:14–15.) Our Lord's appearance was but the beginning of the realization of his promise given three years earlier: "And inasmuch as my people build a house unto me in the name of the Lord, and do not suffer any unclean thing to come into it, that it be not defiled, my glory shall rest upon it; yea, and my presence shall be there, for I will come into it, and all the pure in heart that shall come into it shall see God" (D&C 97:15–16). Jesus Christ accepted the offering of his Saints—this temple built at great sacrifice—and expanded their vision in regard to the importance of that which they had accomplished: "Yea the hearts of thousands and tens of thousands shall greatly rejoice in consequence of the blessings which shall be poured out, and the endowment with which my servants have been endowed in this house" (D&C 110:9).

Moses and the Keys of Gathering

Joseph Smith recorded, "After this vision [of the Savior] closed, the heavens were again opened unto us; and Moses appeared before us, and committed unto us the keys of the gathering of Israel from the four parts of the earth, and the leading of the ten tribes from the land of the north" (D&C 110:11). The keys or directing power restored by the ancient lawgiver enabled the Saints to accomplish the directive delivered in September of 1830, "And ye are called to bring to pass the gathering of mine elect; for mine elect hear my voice and harden not their hearts" (D&C 29:7). To the President of The Church of Jesus Christ of Latter-day Saints —the man appointed "to preside over the whole church, and to be like unto Moses" (D&C 107:91)—were given keys to gather modern Israel. Even as Moses led ancient Israel out of Egyptian bondage, so the President of the Church was given keys to call and lead modern Israel out of the bondage and throes of modern Egypt (see D&C 103:16–20).

People are gathered first spiritually and then temporally. They are gathered first as they accept the true Messiah and are "restored to the true church and fold of God" (2 Nephi 9:2); second, they are gathered as they congregate to the places where the Saints of God are. Only through the eventual establishment of stakes throughout the world could the full concept of Zion be realized; only then will the full blessings of the temple be had by all peoples. Joseph Smith taught, "The main object [of gathering] was to build unto the Lord a house whereby He could reveal unto His people the ordinances of His house and the glories of His Kingdom, and teach the people the way of salvation."[7]

Elias and the Keys of Eternal Marriage

"After this, Elias appeared, and committed the dispensation of the gospel of Abraham, saying that in us and our seed all generations after us should be blessed" (D&C 110:12). The identity of Elias—whether he be Melchizedek, Abraham himself, or a prophet named Elias from the days of Abraham—is not clearly known.[8] This heavenly messenger restored the keys necessary to establish the ancient patriarchal order, making Joseph Smith and the faithful Saints who receive celestial marriage heirs to the blessings and "promises made to the fathers"—Abraham, Isaac, and Jacob.[9] The promises to Joseph Smith (and all worthy Latter-day Saints after him) are glorious: "And as I said unto Abraham concerning the kindreds of the earth, even so I say unto my servant Joseph: In thee and in thy seed shall the kindred of the earth be blessed" (D&C 124:58; cf. 132:30–32).

Elias thus restored the power by which eternal family units are organized through the new and everlasting covenant of marriage. "As the crowning cause for wonderment," Elder Bruce R. McConkie has explained: "God who is no respecter of persons has given a like promise [to that of Abraham and Joseph Smith] to every [member] in the kingdom who has gone to the holy temple and entered into the blessed order of matrimony there performed. Every person married in the temple for time and for all eternity has sealed upon him, conditioned upon his faithfulness, all of the blessings of the ancient patriarchs, including the crowning promise and assurance of eternal increase, which means, literally, a posterity as numerous as the dust particles of the earth."[10]

Elijah and the Sealing Power

The Prophet Joseph Smith wrote concerning the final angelic ministrant on this occasion in the Kirtland Temple: "After this vision had closed, another great and glorious vision burst upon us; for Elijah the prophet, who was taken to heaven without tasting death, stood before us, and said: Behold, the time has fully come, which was spoken of by the mouth of Malachi—testifying that he [Elijah] should be sent, before the great and dreadful day of the Lord come—To turn the hearts of the fathers to the children, and the children to the fathers, lest the whole earth be smitten with a curse" (D&C 110:13–15). Precisely on the day that Elijah's appearance took place, Jews throughout the world were engaged in the celebration of the Passover. Since the time of Malachi—from about 400 B.C.—Jews worldwide waited with anxious anticipation for the coming of Elijah. Elijah did come, but not to Jewish homes; he came rather to a synagogue of the Saints, and to his legal administrators on earth. There he bestowed keys of inestimable worth.

When Moroni appeared to Joseph Smith in 1823 he quoted numerous passages from the Old and New Testaments. The Prophet indicated in his official history that Moroni quoted Malachi 4:5–6 but gave a different rendering from that of the King James text. Malachi (from whom this promise came), we learn by revelation, "had his eye fixed on the restoration of the priesthood" (D&C 128:17). The prophecy began: "Behold, I will reveal unto you the Priesthood, by the hand of Elijah the prophet, before the coming of the great and dreadful day of the Lord" (Joseph Smith—History 1:38; D&C 2:1). Joseph and Oliver had been ordained to the Melchizedek Priesthood and given apostolic power and commission as early as 1829. How was it, then, that Elijah would reveal the priesthood? Simply stated, Elijah was sent to restore the keys of the patriarchal order of priesthood, rights which had not yet been fully operational in this dispensation. Elijah restored the keys whereby families (organized in the patriarchal order through the keys delivered by Elias) could be bound and sealed for eternity.

Three months before his death, Joseph Smith instructed the Latter-day Saints concerning the mission of Elijah: "The spirit, power, and calling of Elijah is, that ye have power to hold the key of the revelations, ordinances, oracles, powers

and endowments of the fulness of the Melchizedek Priesthood and of the kingdom of God on the earth."[11] Elijah
restored the keys whereby individuals and families may
(through the blessings of the holy temple) develop line upon
line to the point where they receive the fulness of the priesthood, and thus become kings and priests, queens and priest-
esses unto God in the patriarchal order. "Those holding the
fulness of the Melchizedek Priesthood," Joseph had taught
earlier, "are kings and priests of the Most High God, holding
the keys of power and blessings."[12] Through the powers
delivered by Elias (the order of marriage entered into by the
fathers—Abraham, Isaac, and Jacob) eternal family units are
created—here and hereafter. Through the powers delivered
by Elijah, man and wife may be sealed unto eternal life, inasmuch as "the power of Elijah is sufficient to make our calling and election sure."[13]

Elijah came to "plant in the hearts of the children the
promises made to the fathers" whereby the "hearts of the
children [should] turn to their fathers" (Joseph Smith—History 1:39; D&C 2:2). The Spirit of the Lord witnesses to
faithful Latter-day Saints of the central place of eternal marriage and of the sublime joys associated with the everlasting
continuation of the family. Through temples, God's promises to the fathers—the promises pertaining to the gospel,
the priesthood, and eternal increase (see Abraham 2:8–11)
—are extended to all the faithful Saints of all ages. The hearts
of the children turn to the ancient fathers because the
children are now participants in and recipients of the blessings of the fathers. Being profoundly grateful for such privileges, members of the Church (motivated by the *spirit* of
Elijah) also find their hearts turning to their more immediate
fathers, and do all within their power (through genealogical
research and the attendant temple work) to ensure that the
blessings of Abraham, Isaac, and Jacob are enjoyed by ancestry as well as posterity. "If it were not so [that is, if Elijah had
not come], the whole earth would be utterly wasted at
[Christ's] coming." (Joseph Smith—History 1:39; D&C 2:3.)
Why? Because the earth would not have accomplished its

foreordained purposes, to establish on its face a family system patterned after the order of heaven. If there were no binding and sealing powers whereby families could be cemented forever, then the earth would never "answer the end of its creation" (D&C 49:16). It would be wasted and cursed, for all men would be forever without root or branch.

Because Elijah came, all other ordinances for the living and the dead (such as baptisms, confirmations, ordinations) have real meaning and are of efficacy, virtue, and force in eternity.[14] The ordinances associated with the ministry of Elijah (centering in temples) are the "capstone blessings" of the gospel and the consummation of the work of the Church; they provide purpose and perspective for all other gospel principles and ordinances.

Salvation: A Family Affair

Marriage in the Resurrection

Much has been made by critics of Mormonism about our belief that marriage and the family unit were intended by God to be eternal. The standard scriptural text used by way of objection comes from Jesus' confrontation with the Sadducees. These Jews baited him in the temple with a question about a woman and her marriage in the resurrection, one who had been wife to seven brothers, seeking through each union to raise up seed to the first after his death. Christ responded by saying: "Ye do err, not knowing the scriptures, nor the power of God. For in the resurrection they neither marry, nor are given in marriage, but are as the angels of God in heaven." (Matthew 22:23–30.) The text in no way says what our critics would like to have it say. First of all, these same people tell us that the Bible is complete and that there is nothing to be added to it. If the Bible is complete, where in the scriptures can we look to find anything other than our present text that could be used to suggest that there is no marriage in heaven or that marriages cannot be performed after the resurrection? The plain fact of the matter is that there is no such text in any scriptural record, be it ancient or modern. And what of the present text? We ask, is a doctrine of the kingdom, a doctrine so essential to our understanding of eternal life, to be established from a single text? Do we credit our knowledge of this doctrine to the wickedness and unbelief of the Sadducees, without which we would have no intelligence on the matter? Is this how such vital theological truths are to come?

To properly understand the present scriptural text, one need only ask the standard question in scriptural interpretation: To whom is the text directed? To whom is Christ speaking? The answer to this query in the specific instance is directed to the Sadducees, a religious sect that rejected Christ, his gospel, his priesthood, and even the doctrine of resurrection. In broader terms, the text applies to all others who reject the gospel of Jesus Christ and its sealing powers. None such have any claim upon a sealing bond between marriage partners or in the family unit. The modern equivalent would be for a person who does not believe in the resurrection to ask the President of the Church which of the seven men to whom she has been married will be her husband in the world to come. The answer, obviously, is none of them. Because one unbeliever has been told that she has no claim upon spouse or family in the world to come, certainly is not to say that those in the household of faith have no such promise; nor does it constitute a doctrinal justification for the idea that no resurrected beings can be married, or that other gospel ordinances cannot be performed for people after they have been resurrected. "And for that matter, there is no revelation, either ancient or modern, which says there is neither marrying nor giving in marriage in heaven itself for righteous people. All that the revelations set forth is that such is denied to the Sadducees and other worldly and ungodly people."[15]

As Latter-day Saints, we have been blessed with a revelation in which the Savior explained to the Prophet Joseph Smith what he intended in his response to these Sadduceean hecklers.

And everything that is in the world, whether it be ordained of men, by thrones, or principalities, or powers, or things of name, whatsoever they may be, that are not by me or by my word, saith the Lord, shall be thrown down, and shall not remain after men are dead, neither in nor after the resurrection, saith the Lord your God.

For whatsoever things remain are by me; and whatsoever things are not by me shall be shaken and destroyed.

Therefore, if a man marry him a wife in the world, and he marry her not by me nor by my word, and he covenant with her so long as he is in the world and she with him, their covenant and marriage are not of force when they are dead, and when they are out of the world; therefore, they are not bound by any law when they are out of the world.

Therefore, when they are out of the world they neither marry nor are given in marriage; but are appointed angels in heaven, which angels are ministering servants, to minister for those who are worthy of a far more, and an exceeding, and an eternal weight of glory.

For these angels did not abide my law; therefore, they cannot be enlarged, but remain separately and singly, without exaltation, in their saved condition, to all eternity; and from henceforth are not gods, but are angels of God forever and ever. (D&C 132:13–17)

The Family Unit Beyond the Veil

Paul said, "I bow my knees," as do we all, "unto the Father of our Lord Jesus Christ, of whom the whole family in heaven and earth is named" (Ephesians 3:14–15). In a manifestation to Brigham Young after his death, Joseph Smith told his successor to be sure to instruct the Saints to keep the Spirit of the Lord, promising that if they would do so, "they will find themselves just as they were organized by our Father in Heaven before they came into the world. Our Father in Heaven organized the human family, but they are all disorganized and in great confusion." Brigham also said that Joseph showed him the pattern, "how they were in the beginning." He said that he could not describe it but that there must yet be "a perfect chain from Father Adam to his latest posterity."[16]

During an illness, Jedediah M. Grant visited the spirit world two nights in succession. He reported a perfect order and government that existed there, saying that the "righteous gathered together," that there were "no wicked spirits among them," and that they were "organized in family capacities." "To my astonishment," he said, "when I looked at families there was a deficiency in some, there was a lack, for I saw families that would not be permitted to come and dwell together, because they had not honored their calling here."[17]

Emphasizing that we must honor our callings and keep our covenants in order to preserve the family unit, Joseph F. Smith said:

> If we live and turn away from truth we will be separated throughout the countless ages of eternity from the society of those we love. We will have no claim upon them, and they will have no claim upon us. There will be an impassable gulf between us over which we can not pass, one to the other. If we die in the faith, having lived righteous lives, we are Christ's, we have the assurance of eternal reward, being in possession of the principles of eternal truth and shall be clothed with glory, immortality and eternal lives. While we sojourn in the flesh we pass a great portion of our life in sorrow; death separates us for a short time, some of us pass behind the vail, but the time will come when we will meet with those who have gone, and enjoy each others' society forever. The separation is but for a moment as it were. No power can separate us then. God having joined us together, we have a claim upon each other—an undeniable claim—inasmuch as we have been united by the power of the priesthood in the Gospel of Christ. Therefore it is better to be separated in this life for a little season, although we have to pass through deprivation, sorrow, trouble, toil, widowhood, orphanage, and many other vicissitudes, than to be separated for all eternity.
>
> By complying with the principles of the Gospel we become heirs of God and joint heirs with Jesus Christ. The anticipation of these great privileges brings happiness to us now, and strengthens our hopes of exaltation and eternal reward in the kingdom of God hereafter. No other power but

that of God, through the knowledge of truth, can give such enjoyment, peace of mind, consolation and happiness to the sorrowing hearts of mortals. The Gospel has been revealed for the salvation and exaltation of the children of men, and if they would only receive it, it would bring, finally, unalloyed and perfect happiness to all, even a "fullness of joy."[18]

Temple and Missionary Work Are One and the Same

"I hope to see us dissolve the artificial boundary line we so often place between missionary work and temple and genealogical work," said President Spencer W. Kimball, "because it is the same great redemptive work."[19] Some years ago a member of the Presiding Bishopric had a son killed in a tragic train accident. Immediately after his death he attempted to visit his father at his Church office but was unable to interrupt him. President McKay often told this story to illustrate that it is possible for us to become too preoccupied with our own matters. Twice the young man appeared to his mother who had been inconsolable over his death. On the second visit he told her that he had been assigned work in his priesthood quorum and "was very busy working with his grandparents and relatives. He told her not to worry about him anymore, because this was the last time that he would be permitted to come back to see her."[20] Wilford Woodruff lost a son in a drowning accident. "I asked the Lord," President Woodruff said, "why he was taken from me. The answer to me was, 'You are doing a great deal for the redemption of your dead; but the law of redemption requires some of your own seed in the spirit world to attend to work connected with this.' That was a new principle to me; but it satisfied me why he was taken away."[21]

Conclusion

As the morning stars sang together for joy at the announcement of the plan of salvation, so the world of the spirits rang forth with refrains of hallelujah with the restoration of knowledge and powers by which the dead are redeemed. A welding link has been established between the fathers and the children, between the heavens and the earth, all that men and earth might answer the ends of their creation. Temples have been erected and men and women are again invited to stand in the divine presence and participate in those sacred ceremonies by which families are forged into eternal units. Thus, the chorus of Latter-day Saints raise their voices in harmony with the words of their Prophet: "Brethren, shall we not go on in so great a cause? Go forward and not backward. Courage, brethren; and on, on to the victory! Let your hearts rejoice, and be exceedingly glad. Let the earth break forth into singing. *Let the dead speak forth anthems of eternal praise to the King Immanuel, who hath ordained, before the world was, that which would enable us to redeem them out of their prison; for the prisoners shall go free.*" (D&C 128:22; italics added.)

8

When Children Die

Behold I say unto you that this thing shall ye teach—
repentance and baptism unto those who are accountable and
capable of committing sin. . . . But little children are alive in
Christ, even from the foundation of the world.

—Moroni 8:10–12

Little children shall live! What more perfect evidence of an omniscient and all-loving God than the doctrine which proclaims that little children who die are heirs of celestial glory! From these no blessing shall be withheld and from such no opportunities will be denied. The testimony of the Book of Mormon and the latter-day oracles is certain and clear: children who die before the time of accountability shall come forth in the resurrection of the just and go on to enjoy all of the privileges associated with eternal life and the family unit.

As a result of his Vision of the Celestial Kingdom, the Prophet Joseph Smith recorded, "I also beheld that all children who die before they arrive at the years of accountability are saved in the celestial kingdom of heaven" (D&C 137:10). This idea was not entirely new to the Prophet, for he had learned from the Book of Mormon and previous revelations of the Lord's disposition in regard to the status of children. An angel explained to King Benjamin that "the infant perisheth not that dieth in his infancy" (Mosiah 3:18). After having described the nature of those who come forth in the first resurrection, Abinadi said simply, "And little children also have eternal life" (Mosiah 15:25). A revelation given in September of 1830 specified that "little children are redeemed from the foundation of the world through mine Only Begotten" (D&C 29:46). In the pages that follow we will turn to the words and counsel of the scriptures and living prophets to provide answers to the most often asked questions associated with this glorious doctrine.

What of Original Sin?

Nephi beheld in vision that because plain and precious truths would be taken away or kept back from the earliest biblical records, "an exceedingly great many" people would stumble and fall, and many thereby would wander in doctrinal darkness, eventually becoming subject to the snares of Satan (1 Nephi 13:20–42). Some of the most critical verities of salvation to be lifted or twisted from their pristine purity are the truths dealing with the Creation, the Fall, and the Atonement. If by no other means, we know that such matters were taught more plainly in the early ages of this world by virtue of the clarity and power in which they are proclaimed and stressed in the Book of Mormon and the Joseph Smith Translation of the Bible. A misunderstanding of the nature of the fall of Adam, for example, has led to some of the most serious heresies and perversions in religious history. Without the exalting knowledge of such matters as the Fall as a foreordained act, a God-inspired and predesigned plan for the perpetuation and preservation of the human family—parent to the atonement of Christ—men struggle helplessly to find meaning in the involvement of our first parents in Eden. Others allegorize or spiritualize away the plain meanings of the scriptures regarding the Fall, and thus cloud in mystery the true purposes behind the Atonement. When revelation is wanting, when unillumined man seeks for understanding of heavenly and eternal matters, he is left to his own resources—to the powers of reason and the limitations of the human intellect.

One of the most influential philosopher-theologians in Christian history was St. Augustine (350–430), a man whose writings and teachings have had a marked impact on the formulation of both Catholic and Protestant beliefs. A historian's description of Augustine's thought on the doctrine of "original sin" follows:

> . . . the first man, Adam, set the pattern for all future life of men. Adam, he taught, committed sin and thus *handed on to all men the effects of this sin. He corrupted the entire human race,* so that all men are condemned to sin for all times. *Adam's sin, therefore, is hereditary.* But God can reform corrupted man by his grace. . . .
>
> Thus *man,* a creation of the all-ruling power of the universe, created out of nothing, *inherits the weaknesses and sins of the first man.* He must pay the price for this sin. But the all-ruling can and does select some men for forgiveness and leaves others to the natural results of Adam's sins. Man is lost forever unless the Creator of the universe chooses to save him.[1]

Paraphrasing Elder James E. Talmage's description of the creeds of Christendom, it would be difficult to have postulated more error in fewer words. We are left to wonder if, in so writing, Augustine has not indeed committed the original (doctrinal) sin! The false doctrine of original sin is thus based upon the notion that Adam and Eve's disobedience was an act of overt rebellion against the Almighty, an attempt to usurp the knowledge available only to the Gods.

How much more ennobling and soul-satisfying is the true doctrine of the Fall, the assurance that Adam—also known as Michael, the prince and archangel—"fell that men might be; and men are, that they might have joy" (2 Nephi 2:25). How much more gratifying it is to know that through the atonement of Christ, the act of redemption on the part of the "Lamb slain from the foundation of the world" (Revelation 13:8), "men will be punished for their own *sins,* and not for Adam's *transgression"* (Articles of Faith 1:2; italics added).[2] One wonders what a difference it would make to a confused Christianity if the following simple yet profound truths from Joseph Smith's translation of Genesis had not been lost from the Bible:

> And [God] called upon our father Adam by his own voice, saying: I am God; I made the world, and men before they were in the flesh.
>
> And he also said unto him: If thou wilt turn unto me, and hearken unto my voice, and believe, and repent of all thy transgressions, and be baptized, even in water, in the name of mine Only Begotten Son, who is full of grace and truth, which is Jesus Christ, the only name which shall be given under heaven, whereby salvation shall come unto the children of men, ye shall receive the gift of the Holy Ghost, asking all things in his name, and whatsoever ye shall ask, it shall be given you.
>
> And our father Adam spake unto the Lord, and said: Why is it that men must repent and be baptized in water? And the Lord said unto Adam: *Behold I have forgiven thee thy transgression in the Garden of Eden.*
>
> Hence came the saying abroad among the people, that the *Son of God hath atoned for original guilt, wherein the sins of the parents cannot be answered upon the heads of the children, for they are whole from the foundation of the world.* (Moses 6:51–54; italics added)

An equally vicious falsehood which follows on the heretical heels of original sin is the moral depravity of man and his complete inability to choose good over evil. As an illustration, we again cite the notions of Augustine:

> The conception of individual freedom was denied by Saint Augustine. According to him, mankind was free in Adam, but since *Adam* chose to sin, he *lost freedom not only for himself, but for all men and for all time. Now no one is free, but all are bound to sin, are slaves of evil.*
>
> But God makes a choice among men of those whom he will save and those whom he will permit to be destroyed because of sin. This choice is not influenced by an act of an individual man, but is determined only by what God wants.

In Augustine we find both fatalism and predestination as far as the individual man is concerned. With Adam there was no fatalism. He was free. But God knew even then how Adam would act, knew he would sin. Thus, from the beginning God made up his mind whom he would save. These were predestined from the first to salvation, and all the rest were predestined to eternal punishment.[3]

Reasoning of this sort surely came from reading such passages as Romans 7 without the clarifying lenses provided by the Prophet Joseph Smith. To read this particular chapter in the New Testament, for example, is to conclude that Paul the Apostle (and thus all men by extension) is a depraved and helpless creature who muddles in sin as a result of carnal nature, an evildoer with little or no hope of deliverance. The Joseph Smith Translation of Romans 7 presents a significantly different picture of Paul and of all men; it might well be called "Paul: Before and After the Atonement," or "The Power of Christ to Change Men's Souls." The King James Version has Paul introspecting as follows: "I am carnal, sold under sin. For that which I do I allow not: for what I would, that do I not; but what I hate, that do I." Further, "For I know that in me (that is, in my flesh,) dwelleth no good thing: for to will is present with me; but how to perform that which is good I find not." (Romans 7:14–15, 18.) The JST lays stress where Paul surely intended it: upon the fact that through the atonement of Christ man is made free from the pull and stain of sin. "When I was under the law [of Moses], I was yet carnal, sold under sin. *But now I am spiritual; for that which I am commanded to do, I do; and that which I am commanded not to allow, I allow not. For what I know is not right I would not do; for that which is sin, I hate."* Finally, "For I know that in me, that is, in my flesh, dwelleth no good thing; for to will is present with me, but to perform that which is good I find not, *only in Christ."* (JST Romans 7:14–16, 19; italics added.) The testimony of Lehi is a confirming witness to this principle of truth: "Adam fell that men might be; and men are, that they might have joy. And the Messiah cometh in the fulness of time, that he may redeem the children of men from the fall. And *because that they are redeemed from the fall they have become free forever, knowing good from evil; to act for themselves and not be acted upon."* (2 Nephi 2:25–26; italics added; cf. Helaman 14:30.)

What of Infant Baptism?

One who chooses to believe in the depravity of man via transmission of the "original sin" is only a stone's throw removed from a practice which would absolve man from the supposed stain of Eden as early as possible. Infant baptism is thus the result of a major doctrinal misunderstanding, a lack of appreciation for the full impact of Christ's atonement upon mankind. A form of the heretical practice seems to pre-date the Christian era by many centuries. The Lord Jehovah spoke to his servant Abraham of a number of the theological errors of the day, some of which appear to be tied to ignorance of the true nature and scope of the Atonement.

> And it came to pass, that Abram fell on his face, and called upon the name of the Lord.
>
> And God talked with him, saying, My people have gone astray from my precepts, and have not kept mine ordinances, which I gave unto their fathers;
>
> *And they have not observed mine anointing, and the burial, or baptism wherewith I commanded them;*
>
> But have turned from the commandment, and *taken unto themselves the washing of children,* and the blood of sprinkling;
>
> And have said that the blood of the righteous Abel was shed for sins;[4] and *have not known wherein they are accountable before me.* (JST Genesis 17:3–7; italics added)

This passage clearly demonstrates the inseparable relationship between atonement and accountability. Simply stated, the atonement of Jesus Christ—the greatest act of love and intercession in all eternity—defines the bounds and limits of accountability. One of the unconditional benefits of the Atonement is the fact that no man or woman will be held responsible for or denied blessings related to a law whose adoption and application were beyond their power. This is the principle which underlies the doctrine concerning the salvation of little children who die. They are simply not accountable for their deeds and therefore are not required as children to participate in those gospel ordinances prepared for accountable persons.

The question of the innocence of children was also a matter which arose in discussions between the Christians and the Jews in the meridian of time. Paul emphasized that the law of circumcision and "the tradition [should] be done away, which saith that little children are unholy; for it was had among the Jews" (D&C 74:6). Joseph Smith's translation of the Bible is a witness that Jesus had taught concerning the innocent status of children. "Take heed that ye despise not one of these little ones," the Master said, "for I say unto you, That in heaven their angels [spirits] do always behold the face of my Father which is in heaven. For the Son of man is come to save that which was lost and to call sinners to repentance; but *these little ones have no need of repentance, and I will save them.*" (JST Matthew 18:10–11; italics added; cf. 19:13.)

During the period of the Great Apostasy (after the first century of the Christian era) the doctrine of infant baptism again reared its ugly head. Elder James E. Talmage has written, "There is no authentic record of infant baptism having been practised during the first two centuries after Christ, and the custom probably did not become general before the fifth century; from the time last named until the Reformation, however, it was accepted by the dominant church organization."[5] Elsewhere Elder Talmage observed:

> Not only was the form of the baptismal rite radically changed [during the time of the apostasy], but the application of the ordinance was perverted. The practice of administering baptism to infants was recognized as orthodox in the third century and was doubtless of earlier origin. In a prolonged disputation as to whether it was safe to postpone the baptism

of infants until the eighth day after birth—in deference to the Jewish custom of performing circumcision on that day—it was generally decided that such delay would be dangerous, as jeopardizing the future well-being of the child should it die before attaining the age of eight days, and that baptism ought to be administered as soon after birth as possible.[6]

It is worth noting that this diabolical doctrine had been introduced in the Americas by approximately the same period. Mormon, in writing to his son Moroni about A.D. 400, delivered a scathing denunciation of the heresy and of those who propound and perpetuate it. The word of the Lord to Mormon was straightforward: "Listen to the words of Christ, your Redeemer, your Lord and your God. Behold, I came into the world not to call the righteous but sinners to repentance; the whole need no physician, but they that are sick [cf. Mark 2:17]; wherefore, little children are whole, for they are not capable of committing sin [cf. D&C 29:47; 74:7]; wherefore the curse of Adam is taken from them in me, that it hath no power over them; and the law of circumcision is done away in me." (Moroni 8:8.) Expounding upon the Lord's words, Mormon reasoned as follows (from Moroni 8):

1. It is solemn mockery before God to baptize children; to do so is to deny the mercies and atoning power of Christ, as well as the power of the Holy Spirit (vv. 9, 20, 23).

2. The leaders of the true church should teach of the necessity of repentance and baptism for those who are accountable and capable of committing sin (v. 10).

3. The leaders of the Church should teach parents that they must repent and be baptized, and humble themselves as their little children (v. 10).

4. The ordinance of baptism appropriately follows the principle of repentance. Since little children, through Christ, are in no need of repentance, they are in no need of baptism. (vv. 11, 19, 25.)

5. Little children are alive in Christ—free from the sins of the sinful world (vv. 12, 22).

6. Any who suppose that children are in need of baptism are devoid of faith (v. 14).

7. Because a belief in infant baptism evidences a significant departure from the faith of Jesus Christ, any who continue in this belief shall perish eventually as pertaining to the things of righteousness (v. 16).

Joseph Smith summarized the issue of infant baptism concisely: "The doctrine of baptizing children, or sprinkling them, or they must welter in hell, is a doctrine not true, not supported in Holy Writ, and is not consistent with the character of God."[7]

Why Do Some Children Die and Others Live?

Lacking a memory of what went before and in some cases having only a general outline of what will come hereafter, we as Latter-day Saints are not in a position to provide all of the answers to all of the questions that might arise. We rest secure in the knowledge that God is our Father, that he is intimately acquainted with each of us, that he knows the end from the beginning and that he will arrange premortal, mortal, and postmortal conditions for our eternal best interest. We rest secure in the knowledge that God knows what is best for each of us, and that he will bring to pass those conditions which will maximize our growth and further our opportunities for exaltation. "We must assume that the Lord knows and arranges beforehand who shall be taken in infancy and who shall remain on earth to undergo whatever tests are needed in their cases."[8]

An eye of faith provides us with a heavenly perspective, a divinely discriminating view of things as God sees them. Joseph the Seer asked, "Why is it that infants, innocent children, are taken away from us, especially those that seem to be the most intelligent and interesting?" He reflected upon the waywardness of the world and provided at least a partial answer to this most difficult question: "The strongest reasons that present themselves to my mind are these: This world is a very wicked world; and it is a proverb that the 'world grows weaker and wiser'; if that is the case, the world grows more wicked and corrupt. In the earlier ages of the world a righteous man, and a man of God and of telligence, had a better chance to do good, to be believed and received than at the present day; but in these days such a man is opposed and persecuted by most of the inhabitants of the earth, and he has much sorrow to pass through here." Then, evidencing the perspective of those who see with the eye of faith, the Prophet added, *"The Lord takes many away even in infancy, that they may escape the envy of man, and the sorrows and evils of this present world; they were too pure, too lovely, to live on earth; therefore, if rightly considered, instead of mourning we have reason to rejoice as they are delivered from evil, and we shall soon have them again."* Finally, Joseph concluded: "The only difference between the old and young dying is, one lives longer in heaven and eternal light and glory than the other, and is freed a little sooner from this miserable wicked world. Notwithstanding all this glory, we for a moment lose sight of it, and mourn the loss, but we do not mourn as those without hope."[9]

In commenting upon the Prophet's remarks, Elder Bruce R. McConkie said: "There are certain spirits who come into this life only to receive bodies; for reasons that we do not know, but which are known in the infinite wisdom of the Eternal Father, they do not need the testing, probationary experiences of mortality. We come here for two great reasons—the first, to get a body; the second, to be tried, examined, schooled, and tested under mortal circumstances, to take a different type of probationary test than we underwent in the pre-mortal life. There are some of the children of our Father, however, who come to earth to get a body—for that reason solely. They do not need the testings of this mortality."[10]

What of the Mentally Deficient?

What is to become of those who are not capable of distinguishing completely between good and evil, those who never come to comprehend sin and grasp the miracle of forgiveness through the atoning blood of Christ? What is the disposition of the Lord with regard to those who never arrive mentally at the age of accountability, those who are in some way deficient in understanding of these vital matters? The revelations of the Restoration are not silent here. To six elders of the Church in September of 1830 the Lord explained: "Little children are redeemed from the foundation of the world through mine Only Begotten; wherefore, they cannot sin, for power is not given unto Satan to tempt little children, until they begin to become accountable before me; for it is given unto them even as I will, according to mine own pleasure, that great things may be required at the hand of their fathers." All who have knowledge have been commanded to repent. Of them who have "no understanding" the Lord has said: *"And he that hath no understanding, it remaineth in me to do according as it is written."* (D&C 29:46–50; italics added; cf. D&C 68:25–28.)

Elder Bruce R. McConkie has written the following concerning the status of the mentally deficient: "It is with them as it is with little children. They never arrive at the years of accountability and are considered as though they were little children. If because of some physical deficiency, or for some other reason unknown to us, they never mature in the spiritual or moral sense, then they never become accountable for sins. They need no baptism; they are alive in Christ; and they will receive, inherit, and possess in eternity on the same basis as do all children."[11]

Will Children Who Die Ever Be Tested?

Let us reason on this matter, leaning heavily upon the wisdom of the prophets for support. We have attempted to demonstrate heretofore that a righteous man or woman cannot take a backward step spiritually after death; in short, the righteous have completed their days of probation in mortality. It was Amulek who informed us that our disposition here will be our disposition hereafter (see Alma 34:32–35). Such is the case with regard to little children. They were pure in this existence, will be pure in the world of spirits, and will come forth in the resurrection of the pure in heart at the appropriate time. At the time of the second coming of Christ, wickedness will be cleansed from the face of the earth. The great Millennium will be ushered in with power, and then Satan and his hosts will be bound by the righteousness of the people. (See 1 Nephi 22:26.) During this glorious era of enlightenment, the earth shall be given to the righteous "for an inheritance; and they shall multiply and wax strong, and *their children shall grow up without sin unto salvation"* (D&C 45:58; italics added). But will not the devil be loosed at the end of the Millennium, some may ask? Could not those who had left mortality without trial be tested during that "little season"? Certainly not, we answer, for these children will already have come forth from the graves as resurrected and immortal beings. How could such persons—whose salvation is already assured—possibly be tested? To reason otherwise is to place God and all exalted beings in peril of apostasy. In the words of President Joseph Fielding Smith, "Satan will be loosed to gather his forces after the millennium. The people who will be tempted, will be people living on this earth, and they will have every opportunity to accept the gospel or reject it. Satan will have nothing to do whatever with little children, or grown people who have received their resurrection and entered into the celestial kingdom. *Satan cannot tempt little children in this life, nor in the spirit world, nor after the resurrection. Little children who die before reaching the years of accountability will not be tempted."*[12]

At this point it is helpful to consider the tender words of Mormon: "Behold, I speak with boldness, having authority from God; and I fear not what man can do; for perfect love casteth out all fear. And I am filled with charity, which is everlasting love; wherefore, all children are alike unto me; wherefore, I love little children with a perfect love; and they are all alike and partakers of salvation." (Moroni 8:16–17.) We trust that God will eventually reveal more of the particulars of this doctrine to the Church through his appointed servants in days to come. In the meantime, however, we are under obligation to believe and teach that which we have received from an omniscient and all-loving God.

What Is Children's Status in and After the Resurrection?

It is a marvelous thing to consider that a seer has walked among us, and that seers continue to grace the earth in this final gospel dispensation. We need to feel profoundly grateful to God our Father for sending the Prophet Joseph Smith, one who communed with Jehovah and was schooled in the mysteries of the kingdom of Jehovah. Joseph has brought comfort and consolation and comprehension to man in this day regarding the ever-present phenomenon of death and the little-understood world beyond the grave. In speaking of the status of children in the resurrection, the Prophet taught in 1842: "As concerning the resurrection, I will merely say that *all men will come from the grave as they lie down,* whether old or young; there will not be 'added unto their stature one cubit,' neither taken from it; *all will be raised by the power of God, having spirit in their bodies, and not blood. Children will be enthroned in the presence of God and the Lamb with bodies of the same stature that they had on earth, having been redeemed by the blood of the Lamb; they will there enjoy the fulness of that light, glory and intelligence, which is prepared in the celestial kingdom."*[13] Some two years later, in the Follett discourse, Joseph repeated the same doctrine; he delivered the comforting assurance to grieving parents who had lost little ones that they would again enjoy the companionship of their children; that these tiny ones would not grow in the grave, but they would come forth as they had been laid to rest—as children.[14]

Some confusion arose over the years after the Prophet Joseph Smith's death concerning his teachings on the status of children in the resurrection. Some erroneously claimed that the Prophet taught that children would be resurrected as children and *never* grow, but would remain in that state through all eternity. President Joseph F. Smith collected testimonies and affidavits from a number of persons who had heard the King Follett Sermon, and it was his powerful witness that Joseph Smith Jr., had taught the truth but had been misunderstood by some. President Smith spoke the following in 1895 at the funeral of Daniel W. Grant, the child of Heber J. Grant:

> Under these circumstances, our beloved friends who are now deprived of their little one, have great cause for joy and rejoicing, even in the midst of the deep sorrow that they feel at the loss of their little one for a time. They know he is all right; they have the assurance that their little one has passed away without sin. Such children are in the bosom of the Father. They will inherit their glory and their exaltation, and they will not be deprived of the blessings that belong to them; . . . all that could have been obtained and enjoyed by them if they had been permitted to live in the flesh will be provided for them hereafter. They will lose nothing by being taken away from us in this way.
>
> This is a consolation to me. Joseph Smith, the Prophet, was the promulgator under God of these principles. He was in touch with the heavens. God revealed himself unto him, and made known unto him the principles that lie before us, and which are comprised in the everlasting gospel. Joseph Smith declared that the mother who laid down her little child, being deprived of the privilege, the joy, and the satisfaction of bringing it up to manhood or womanhood in this world, would after the resurrection, have all the joy, satisfaction and pleasure, and even more than it would have been possible to have had in mortality, in seeing her child grow to the full measure of the stature of its spirit. If this be true, and I believe it, what a consolation it is. . . . It matters not whether these tabernacles mature in this world, or have to wait and mature in the world to come, according to the word of the Prophet Joseph Smith, the body will develop, either in time or in eternity, to the full stature of the spirit, and when the mother is deprived of the pleasure and joy of rearing her babe to manhood or womanhood in this life, through the hand of death, that privilege will be renewed to her hereafter, and she will enjoy it to a fuller fruition than it would be possible for

her to do here. When she does it there, it will be with certain knowledge that the results will be without failure; whereas here, the results are unknown until after we have passed the test.[15]

Children will come forth from the grave as children, be raised to maturity by worthy parents, and be entitled to receive all of the ordinances of salvation that eventuate in the everlasting continuation of the family unit.[16]

There are no joys of more transcendent beauty than family joys and no sorrows more poignant than family sorrows. God lives in the family unit and knows family feelings. He has provided a means—through the mediation of his Only Begotten—whereby families may be reunited and affections renewed. "All your losses will be made up to you in the resurrection," the Prophet Joseph Smith declared, "provided you continue faithful. By the vision of the Almighty I have seen it."[17]

Conclusion

In speaking of the fruits of this everlasting principle—the doctrine that little children shall be saved—a modern Apostle has written:

> Truly it is one of the sweetest and most soul-satisfying doctrines of the gospel! It is also one of the greatest evidences of the divine mission of the Prophet Joseph Smith. In his day the fiery evangelists of Christendom were thundering from their pulpits that the road to hell is paved with the skulls of infants not a span long because careless parents had neglected to have their offspring baptized. Joseph Smith's statements, as recorded in the Book of Mormon and latter-day revelation, came as a refreshing breeze of pure truth: *little children shall be saved*. Thanks be to God for the revelations of his mind where these innocent and pure souls are concerned![18]

9

Many Mansions

In my Father's house are many mansions: if it were not so, I would have told you. I go to prepare a place for you.

—John 14:2

Even as all die, so all must rise from the dead, each in his own order, each to his own glory. No righteous deed will go unrewarded and no dark act undetected. The just Paymaster will give to each in full measure, rewarding the small and the great according to their works and the desires of their hearts, even to the granting of all that the Father hath. To the meridian Twelve, as they sat at the Last Supper, Jesus said, "In my Father's house are many mansions: if it were not so, I would have told you" (John 14:2). That is to say, if judgment were not by works and the rewards of eternity as diverse as the works and desires of men, it would be so completely contrary to everything that I have taught you, and to everything in the revealed word, that I would be obligated to announce this great inconsistency to you.

Surely the rewards that come from God will be worthy of the majesty and power of God. It would be ungodly to grant to man that for which he was unworthy; it would be less than godlike for the divine Father of us all to refuse to share all that he had with those who had laid their all upon his altar. A theology that refuses God the right to make of his children joint heirs, and yet expects the sacrifice of all things by mere mortals, is a theology which demands of men greater magnanimity than of God from whom the very virtue is to have come. The glory of God, which is manifest in all that he does, is nowhere more evident than in the order and nature of the resurrection and the eternal rewards granted to his children.

Resurrection

The Bible can be searched in vain for a definition of *resurrection*. Once again it is to the revelations of the Restoration that we must turn to part the veil and know of future eternities. And how simple the matter when the Spirit speaks—*resurrection is the inseparable union of body and spirit.* Amulek stated it thus, "This mortal body is raised to an immortal body, that is from death, even from the first death unto life, that they can die no more; their spirits uniting with their bodies, never to be divided; thus the whole becoming spiritual and immortal, that they can no more see corruption" (Alma 11:45). Or, as Joseph F. Smith declared in his Vision of the Redemption of the Dead, "Their sleeping dust was to be restored unto its perfect frame, bone to his bone, and the sinews and the flesh upon them, the spirit and the body to be united never again to be divided, that they might receive a fulness of joy" (D&C 138:17).

A loving father does not withhold from his children, he does not seek that they be less than he, nor did he choose to father them for the purpose of their becoming his servants. Our God is a corporeal physical being and in the resurrection it is our privilege to become like him. While body and spirit are separated "man cannot receive a fulness of joy" (D&C 93:34); it is in and through the resurrection that such fulness comes. Alma expressed it beautifully: "The soul shall be restored to the body, and the body to the soul; yea, and every limb and joint shall be restored to its body; yea, even a hair of the head shall not be lost; but all things shall be restored to their proper and perfect frame" (Alma 40:23).

The Order of the Resurrections

"For as in Adam all die, even so in Christ shall all be made alive. *But every man in his own order:* Christ the firstfruits; afterward they that are Christ's at his coming." (1 Corinthians 15:22–23; italics added.) Though the resurrection is a free gift to all, men come forth from the grave as they have merited the right—from Jesus Christ, the firstfruits, to those who remain filthy still, or from the most righteous to the least righteous, each man in his appointed time and order.

The First Resurrection or the Morning of the First Resurrection

The scriptural phrases *first resurrection* or *morning of the first resurrection* (which is common to patriarchal blessings) are frequently used interchangeably. The phrases are descriptive of those once in paradise, those who bore the title "just men made perfect," those referred to as the *just* (D&C 76:17), meaning that they are justified, ratified, sealed, or approved of God. These are they to whom the promise has been given that they shall be equal with him in power, might, and dominion (see D&C 76:95). Those coming forth in this resurrection will inherit the celestial kingdom and will enjoy eternal life, which is God's life. Thus the first resurrection is a celestial resurrection.

The Book of Mormon speaks of a *first resurrection* which included the righteous and faithful from the time of Adam to the time that Christ came forth from the grave. Abinadi described it thus: "And there cometh a resurrection, even a first resurrection; yea, even a resurrection of those that have been, and who are, and who shall be, even until the resurrection of Christ—for so shall he be called. And now, the resurrection of all the prophets, and all those that have believed in their words, or all those that have kept the commandments of God, shall come forth in the first resurrection; therefore, they are the first resurrection." (Mosiah 15:21–22.) This *first resurrection* is not to be confused with the first resurrection spoken of in the Doctrine and Covenants, which has reference to the coming forth from the grave of the faithful Saints from the time of Christ to the time of his second coming (see D&C 88:96–98). Those living in the Millennium are also spoken of as coming forth in a first resurrection, for they too obtain an exaltation (see D&C 132:19).

The Afternoon of the First Resurrection

"And after this [the morning of the first resurrection or the sounding of the first trump] another angel shall sound, which is the second trump; and then cometh the redemption of those who are Christ's at his coming; who have received their part in that prison which is prepared for them, that they might receive the gospel, and be judged according to men in the flesh" (D&C 88:99). These are heirs of the terrestrial kingdom, those who accepted Christ but not in that faith that would have exalted them. Of the time of Christ's coming we read, "Then shall the heathen nations be redeemed, and they that knew no law shall have part in the first resurrection; and it shall be tolerable for them" (D&C 45:54). That redemption that requires "no law" (meaning that they have not accepted the gospel) and extends a reward that is "tolerable" cannot be confused with the blessings associated with the morning of the first resurrection as previously described.

The Resurrection of the Unjust

"And again, another trump shall sound, which is the third trump; and then come the spirits of men who are to be judged, and are found under condemnation; and these are the rest of the dead; and they live not again until the thousand years are ended, neither again, until the end of the earth. And another trump shall sound, which is the fourth trump, saying: There are found among those who are to remain until that great and last day, even the end, who shall remain filthy still." (D&C 88:100–102.) After the celestial and terrestrial resurrections, after the thousand years, or the millennial era, has ended, comes the resurrection of the unjust—those who will inherit the telestial kingdom and those who have become the children of perdition. Order still prevails; the telestial resurrection precedes that of those whose wickedness places them beyond the power of Christ's redemption. Even hell cannot purge the filth of those who, having had a sure witness and knowledge of heaven's secrets, have denied all and actively sought to crucify Christ afresh.

The Degrees of Glory

The Savior promised that he would teach the gospel to those who were dead. "The hour is coming," Christ said, "in the which all that are in the graves shall hear his voice, and shall come forth; they that have done good, unto the resurrection of life; and they that have done evil, unto the resurrection of damnation" (John 5:28–29). It was while Joseph Smith and Sidney Rigdon pondered the implications of John's statement that there would be a resurrection of life and a resurrection of damnation, that they received the great vision known to us as the Vision of the Glories. Joseph said: "From sundry revelations which had been received, it was apparent that many important points touching the salvation of man had been taken from the Bible, or lost before it was compiled. It appeared self-evident from what truths were left, that if God rewarded every one according to the deeds done in the body, the term 'Heaven,' as intended for the Saints' eternal home, must include more kingdoms than one."[1] A series of visions were then opened to the eyes of Joseph and Sidney in which they learned of the division of kingdoms, or the degrees of glory, that will exist in the worlds to come. The highest of these kingdoms was called *celestial*, and was likened to the glory of the sun; the next was called *terrestrial*, and was likened to the glory of the moon; and the third, or the lowest of these heavenly glories, was called *telestial,* and was likened to the glory of the stars. We will briefly describe each.

The Celestial Kingdom

In a subsequent revelation Joseph Smith learned that the earth was a living entity, having both body and spirit; that it, like man, would yet die and be resurrected; and that in the resurrection it would be "sanctified from all unrighteousness" and become the kingdom upon which those who were to be exalted would live. "For after it hath filled the measure of its creation, it shall be crowned with glory, even with the presence of God the Father; that bodies who are of the celestial kingdom may possess it forever and ever; for, for this intent," the Lord said, "was it made and created, and for this intent are they sanctified." (D&C 88:17–20, 26.) Thus, to obtain the *celestial kingdom* one must come forth in the morning of the first resurrection and must lay claim in the resurrection to a celestial body. One obtains a celestial body by developing celestial interests, appetites, propensities, desires, attitudes, and inclinations—that is, by living the gospel of Jesus Christ in full. "For he who is not able to abide the law of a celestial kingdom cannot abide a celestial glory" (D&C 88:22).

The celestial kingdom is divided into three heavens or degrees, and in order to obtain the highest, one must be married by the power and authority of the priesthood for time and eternity. Only those who are so married and live true to their marriage covenants continue in the marriage and family relationship in the worlds to come. (D&C 131:1–4.) These become "joint-heirs with Christ" (Romans 8:17), "into whose hands the Father has given all things—they are they who are priests and kings, who have received of his fulness, and of his glory" (D&C 76:55–56), and indeed "are gods, even the sons of God" (D&C 76:58), for they are to be equal with him in power, might, and dominion (D&C 76:95). Describing the nature of their society, Joseph Smith stated that the "same sociality which exists among us here will exist among us there, only it will be coupled with eternal glory, which glory we do not now enjoy" (D&C 130:2). Of the other two degrees, or glories, within the celestial kingdom we know only that their inhabitants did not enter into eternal marriage and thus "remain separately and singly, without exaltation, in their saved condition, to all eternity; and from henceforth are not gods, but are angels of God forever and ever" (D&C 132:17).

The Terrestrial Kingdom

The terrestrial or middle kingdom consists of those who come forth in the afternoon of the first resurrection. Four classes of people are given in the Vision of the Glories to represent the nature of souls that will comprise this kingdom. First, there are those who died without the gospel law and obviously did not accept it when it was taught to them in the world of the spirits (v. 72). Second, there are those who had the opportunity to accept the gospel in this life and did not do so, but did when the opportunity came to them the second time in the spirit world (vv. 73–74). Such are not celestial because they rejected the gospel in mortality in circumstances in which they were obligated to accept it; nonetheless, they are blessed by their acceptance of it in the spirit world in that they can inherit the terrestrial kingdom. Third, there are "honorable men of the earth, who were blinded by the craftiness of men" (v. 75). As moral and honest people they establish the standard for all that inherit the terrestrial glory and show by way of contrast how much more is expected of those who aspire to be celestial. And fourth, "These are they who are not valiant in the testimony of Jesus; wherefore, they obtain not the crown over the kingdom of our God" (v. 79). To be valiant in testimony is to be courageous, brave, bold, or valorous. By implication, this number will embrace many Latter-day Saints who could stand and bear a powerful testimony but who failed to serve with all their "heart, might, mind and strength," and thus did not "stand blameless" in the day of judgment (D&C 4:2). A testimony of the gospel, independent of faithful service, is not sufficient to save one in the kingdom of God.

The Telestial Kingdom

As baptism is the door through which one enters the earthly kingdom of God and the gate to the heavenly kingdom, so hell is the gate to the telestial world. None will inhabit this kingdom who did not first suffer for their own sins in that part of the spirit prison known to us as hell. Having done so, having "paid the uttermost farthing" (Matthew 5:26), they then come forth clean from sin to the least of the kingdoms of glory, but a kingdom of glory nonetheless. Dramatizing the glory of this, the least of God's kingdoms, the revelation states that it "surpasses all understanding" (v. 89). In so saying, it is not the purpose of the Lord to encourage any to seek after or be satisfied with such a glory, but rather to show again by contrast the marvel of the celestial realm and to indicate the mercies and blessings that the Lord will give even to the wicked. Indeed, all that the God of heaven need do to create a world that surpasses all earthly understanding would be to alleviate death, hunger, pain, and evil. Such a state would surely transcend the imagination of men.

Those inheriting the telestial world constitute two major classes. First, there are those who declare allegiance to false religions, who used their pretended devotion to some principle, cause, or prophet, as an excuse to reject the fulness of the gospel when it was brought to them (vv. 99–101). Had their rejection of the gospel not been the result of their unwillingness to repent of their sins, or because they were honestly deceived, they would have come forth in the terrestrial resurrection. The second class of people comprising the telestial kingdom are "liars, and sorcerers, and adulterers, and whoremongers, and whosoever loves and makes a lie," as well as idolaters and murderers (v. 103; Revelation 21:8; 22:15). These are they of whom Alma said, "They have no part nor portion of the Spirit of the Lord; for behold, they chose evil works rather than good" (Alma 40:13). Of these the revelation declares: "Where God and Christ dwell they cannot come, worlds without end" (v. 112).

Conclusion

The reader is reminded that everything that we have been able to say about the nature and order of the resurrection has latter-day revelation as its source. The same is true of all that we know of the various degrees of glory; our knowledge of this doctrine is also entirely dependent on modern revelation. On these matters the Bible as it has come to us is either ambiguous or silent. This is a rather surprising thing, in view of the importance of these doctrines as a source of faith, understanding, comfort, and encouragement. It is even more surprising when it is remembered that the verity of the Christian belief that Jesus is the Christ is fully dependent on the reality of the resurrection. Christianity rises or falls on the doctrine. If there was no resurrection, Jesus of Nazareth was not the Christ and our bodies will be consigned endlessly to mortal dust and our spirits will be forever divorced from the presence of God (see 1 Corinthians 15:12–17).

It is also significant that the testimony of the New Testament disciples of Christ's resurrection, like that of our dispensation, was wholly dependent on revelation. The resurrected Christ manifested himself to "above five hundred brethren" (1 Corinthians 15:6) in the hills of Galilee (Matthew 28:16–18), along with numerous other appearances in the Old World. "Him God raised up the third day, and shewed him openly," Peter testified, "not to all the people, but unto witnesses chosen before of God" (Acts 10:40–41). The system of testifying of Christ in the New World was the same. Again Christ showed himself openly to a multitude, "and the multitude did see and hear and bear record; and they know that their record is true for they all of them did see and hear, every man for himself; and they were in number about two thousand and five hundred souls; and they did consist of men, women, and children" (3 Nephi 17:25).

From the early hours of that Sunday morning, when Christ first appeared to Mary Magdalene and then the other women, to the time of his return, when he will be attended by "ten thousands of his saints" (Jude 1:14), those men, women, and children who bear a proper testimony of him must testify also of the principle of current revelation. We can know Christ and the doctrines of the afterlife in no other way. Our testimony must be one of the opening of the heavens, the manifestation of Christ, the calling of prophets, the dispensing of revelation, and the granting of the gift of the Holy Ghost; the knowledge of Christ and the nature of the worlds to come can be had in no other way. Such is our testimony.

10

The Gift of Salvation

If you keep my commandments and endure to the end you shall have eternal life, which gift is the greatest of all the gifts of God.

—D&C 14:7

Salvation is the greatest of all the gifts of God. It is the rightful inheritance of those who have come to think as God thinks, believe as he believes, act as he acts, and thus experience what he experiences. It entitles such individuals to the power and might of the Eternal Father and thus a joint heirship with Christ the Lord. They become equal with their Master in power, might, and dominion. Such are the promises extended to those of whom the scriptures declare: "Ye are gods; and all of you are children of the most High" (Psalm 82:6).

Immortality and Eternal Life

Immortality

To possess the gift of *immortality* is to have the power to live forever, the capacity to endure every obstacle to life. The scriptures speak expressly of immortality as one of the wondrous gifts to man through the atonement of Jesus

Christ. And yet we recognize that the spirit of man is already an immortal entity, a conscious personality which cannot cease to exist. Even if there had been no Atonement, the spirit of man would live on everlastingly. But the immortality of which the scriptures almost always speak is that immortality associated with the immortal soul or resurrected body—the inseparable union of body and spirit equipped thereafter for a kingdom of glory. Only through the actions of a God—the redemptive labors of Jesus the Messiah—can such an immortal state be attained. "Now if we be dead with Christ," Paul taught, "we believe that we shall also live with him. Knowing that Christ being raised from the dead dieth no more; death hath no more dominion over him. For in that he died, he died unto sin once; but in that he liveth, he liveth unto God." (Romans 6:8–10.)

Spiritual and Immortal

In Amulek's description of the resurrected body, he uses the word *spiritual* synonymously with the word *immortal*. This usage appears to be common to the teachings of the prophets of all ages, given to denote a state which is not subject to death. (Cf. 1 Corinthians 15:44; D&C 88:27; Moses 3:9.) Immortality is a free gift to all men and women who qualified for the second estate, a gift of grace which requires neither righteousness nor rigorous attention to God's laws, "for as in Adam all die, even so in Christ shall all be made alive" (1 Corinthians 15:22). We cannot improve upon Amulek's expression: "Now, *this restoration* [of body and spirit] *shall come to all,* both old and young, both bond and free, both male and female, both the wicked and the righteous" (Alma 11:44; italics added).

Eternal Life

Eternal life is the kind of life enjoyed by our Father in Heaven; it is God's life (see Moses 7:35). It consists primarily of two things: (1) inheriting, receiving, and possessing the fulness of the glory of the Father; and (2) a continuation of the family unit in eternity (see D&C 132:19).

Immortality, as we have indicated, is a free gift to all. Eternal life, on the other hand, is something for which one must qualify through faithful obedience to the statutes and commandments provided through the plan of salvation. Both of these conditions are made available through our Lord's suffering in Gethsemane and on Golgotha, as well as his rise to glorious immortality from the Arimathean's tomb. In a way still incomprehensible to mortal and finite minds, our Savior's conquest of physical death—his bursting the bands and hold of death—passed upon all men: because he rose, so we all will likewise rise, each in his appointed time and order. Immortality, the measure of the *quantity* of an everlasting life, is thus a reality. Also inexplicable is the manner in which our Deliverer descended below all things and took upon him the weight and effects of the sins of all mankind, making repentance and forgiveness available to the penitent. Eternal life, an expression descriptive of the *quality* of one's immortality, is thus also a reality and a possibility for those who accept and apply the principles of the gospel of Jesus Christ.

Having spoken in a modern revelation of the creation and fall of Adam, the Lord observed: "And thus did I, the Lord God, appoint unto man the days of his probation—*that by his natural death he might be raised in immortality unto eternal life, even as many as would believe"* (D&C 29:43; italics added). Paul wrote to Timothy of our Master as he "who hath abolished death, and hath brought [eternal] life and immortality to light through the gospel" (2 Timothy 1:10). Succinctly capsulizing the meaning and purpose and labors of godhood, the Lord said to Moses: "For behold, this is my work and my glory—to bring to pass the immortality and eternal life of man" (Moses 1:39; cf. John 11:25).

Salvation and Exaltation

"Salvation consists in the glory, authority, majesty, power, and dominion which Jehovah possesses and in nothing else; and no being can possess it but himself or one like him."[1] So taught Joseph Smith to the School of the Prophets in the winter of 1834–35. Both the Prophet of the Restoration and Paul the Apostle taught that Christ had gained salvation because he had put all enemies under his feet, the last enemy being death. It is just so with all men.[2]

Salvation is eternal life. It is life in the highest heaven, life among the Gods and the angels. The word *salvation* means exactly the same thing as eternal life, but simply lays stress upon one's saved condition, his state being one of deliverance from death and sin through the atoning sacrifice of Jesus Christ. *Exaltation* is another word with which we have come to identify the glories of the celestial kingdom; exaltation has the same meaning as eternal life; it has the same meaning as salvation. To be saved is to be exalted, the latter term simply laying stress upon the elevated and ennobled status of one who so qualifies to dwell with and be a part of the Church of the Firstborn, the Church of the Exalted. Elder Bruce R. McConkie has written:

> We are ofttimes prone to create artificial distinctions, to say that salvation means one thing and exaltation another, to suppose that salvation means to be resurrected, but that exaltation or eternal life is something in addition thereto. It is true that there are some passages of scripture that use salvation in a special and limited sense in order to give an overall perspective of the plan of salvation that we would not otherwise have. (2 Nephi 9:1–27; D&C 76:40–49; 132:15–17.) These passages show the difference between general or universal salvation that consists in coming forth from the grave in immortality, and specific or individual salvation that consists of an inheritance in the celestial kingdom. . . .
>
> Since it is the prophetic purpose to lead men to full salvation in the highest heaven of the celestial world, *when they speak and write about salvation, almost without exception, they mean eternal life or exaltation. They use the terms salvation, exaltation, and eternal life as synonyms, as words that mean exactly the same thing without any difference, distinction, or variance whatever.*[3]

Amulek certainly equated the two terms *eternal life* and *salvation.* He said concerning the coming of the Messiah,

"And he shall come into the world to redeem his people; and he shall take upon him the transgressions of those who believe on his name; and *these are they that shall have eternal life, and salvation cometh to none else"* (Alma 11:40; italics added). In a revelation given to the Prophet Joseph Smith and Oliver Cowdery, the Savior said, "If thou wilt do good, yea, and hold out faithful to the end, *thou shalt be saved in the kingdom of God, which is the greatest of all the gifts of God; for there is no gift greater than the gift of salvation"* (D&C 6:13; italics added). Two months later the Lord spoke to David Whitmer, "And, if you keep my commandments and endure to the end *you shall have eternal life, which gift is the greatest of all the gifts of God"* (D&C 14:7; italics added).

Eternal marriage is the gate through which those intent upon eternal life must enter. "In the celestial glory there are three heavens or degrees," Joseph Smith explained. "And in order to obtain the highest, a man must enter into this order of the priesthood [meaning the new and everlasting covenant of marriage]; And if he does not, he cannot obtain it. He may enter into the other, but that is the end of his kingdom; he cannot have an increase." (D&C 131:1–4.) The Prophet also taught: "Except a man and his wife enter into an everlasting covenant and be married for eternity, while in this probation, by the power and authority of the Holy Priesthood, they will cease to increase when they die; *that is, they will not have any children after the resurrection.* But those who are married by the power and authority of the priesthood in this life, and continue without committing the sin against the Holy Ghost, will continue to increase and have children in the celestial glory."[4] The scriptures thus speak of one qualifying for the blessing of *eternal lives* (see D&C 132:22–25). To have eternal lives is to possess eternal life in the highest degree of the celestial kingdom, to be worthy of salvation, and to be a candidate for exaltation. The phrase *eternal lives* simply lays stress upon the right of a worthy man and woman to enjoy "the continuation of the seeds," the everlasting perpetuation of the family unit.[5]

Who Then Can Be Saved?

There is no ceiling on the number of saved beings. The design of God's plan is to save all who will be saved. We state as an article of our faith: "We believe that through the Atonement of Christ, *all mankind may be saved,* by obedience to the laws and ordinances of the Gospel" (Articles of Faith 1:3; italics added). No person was promised eternal life in premortality on an unconditional basis, and likewise no soul was condemned as reprobate before the foundations of the earth were laid.[6] In the words of Lehi to his son Jacob, "salvation is free" (2 Nephi 2:4), meaning that it is freely available to all. Our God does not operate by some "secret agenda," for his plan and his purposes are available and accessible to all. Nephi taught that "the Lord God worketh not in darkness." Further, "He doeth not anything save it be for the benefit of the world; for he loveth the world, even that he layeth down his own life that he may draw all men unto him. Wherefore, he commandeth none that they shall not partake of his salvation." Emphatically, Nephi declared: "Hath he commanded any that they should not partake of his salvation? Behold I say unto you, Nay; but he hath given it free for all men; and he hath commanded his people that they should persuade all men to repentance." (2 Nephi 26:23–24, 27.)

Innumerable Hosts to Be Saved

The scriptures speak often of a "strait gate" and a "narrow way" which lead unto that life which we have come to know as eternal life. Stress is frequently placed upon the fact that "few" will ultimately get onto that path and navigate that course which will result in a saved condition hereafter. "Strait is the gate, and narrow the way that leadeth unto the exaltation and the continuation of the lives, and few there be that find it, because ye receive me not in the world neither do ye know me." On the other hand, "broad is the gate, and wide the way that leadeth to the deaths; and many there are that go in thereat, because they receive me not, neither do they abide in my law." (D&C 132:22, 25; cf. Matthew 7:13–14.)

These are scriptural passages which must be viewed in proper perspective. In the long run, we must ever keep in mind that our God and Father is a successful parent, one who will save far more of his children than he will lose! If these words seem startling at first, let us reason for a moment. In comparison to the number of wicked souls *at any given time,* perhaps the numbers of faithful followers seem small. But we must keep in mind how many of our spirit brothers and sisters—almost an infinite number—will be saved. What of the children who died before the age of accountability—billions of little ones from the days of Adam to the time of the Millennium? What of the billions of those who never had opportunity to hear the gospel message in mortality, but who afterwards received the glad tidings, this because of a disposition which hungered and thirsted after righteousness? And, might we ask, What of the innumerable hosts who qualified for exaltation from Enoch's city, from Melchizedek's Salem, or from the golden era of the Nephites? What of the countless billions of those children to be born during the great millennial era—during a time when disease and death have no sting nor victory over mankind? This is that time of which we have spoken already, a season when "children shall grow up without sin unto salvation" (D&C 45:58). Given the renewed and paradisiacal state of the earth, it may well be that more persons will live on the earth during the thousand years of our Lord's reign—persons who are of at least a terrestrial nature—than the combined total of all who have lived during the previous six thousand years of the earth's temporal continuance. Indeed, who can count the number of saved beings in eternity? Our God, who is triumphant in all battles against the forces of evil, will surely be victorious in the numbers of his children who will be saved.

Salvation: A Process

In regard to the Latter-day Saints, it is vital that we have hope, that we point and align and rivet ourselves on that goal of eternal life, this in spite of our imperfections. Gaining salvation and attaining perfection are processes, lengthy processes which will go on even beyond the time of death. (See D&C 93:19.) In short, there are no instant Christians, no sudden disciples. In speaking to the youth of the Church, Elder Bruce R. McConkie taught the following vital lessons:

> We do not work out our salvation in a moment; it doesn't come to us in an instant, suddenly. Gaining salvation is a process. Paul says, "Work out your salvation with fear and trembling" (Philippians 2:12). To some members of the Church who had been baptized and who were on the course leading to eternal life, he said, "Now is our salvation nearer than when we believed" (Romans 13:11). That is, "We have made some progress along the straight and narrow path. We are going forward, and if we continue in that direction, eternal life will be our everlasting reward. . . ."
>
> We say that a man has to be born again, meaning that he has to die as pertaining to the unrighteous things in the world. Paul said, "Crucify the old man of sin and come forth in a newness of life" (Romans 6:6). We are born again when we die as pertaining to unrighteousness and when we live as pertaining to the things of the Spirit. But that doesn't happen in an instant, suddenly. That also is a process. Being born again is a gradual thing, except in a few isolated instances that are so miraculous that they get written up in the scriptures. As far as the generality of the members of the Church are concerned, we are born again by degrees, and we are born again to added light and added knowledge and added desires for righteousness as we keep the commandments. . . .
>
> So it is with the plan of salvation. We have to become perfect to be saved in the celestial kingdom. But nobody becomes perfect in this life. Only the Lord Jesus attained that state, and he had an advantage that none of us has. He was the Son of God, and he came into this life with a spiritual capacity and a talent and an inheritance that exceeded beyond all comprehension what any of the rest of us was born with. Our revelations say that he was like unto God in the premortal life and he was, under the Father, the creator of worlds without number. That Holy Being was the Holy One of Israel anciently

and he was the Sinless One in mortality. This shows that we can strive and go forward toward that goal, but no other mortal—not the greatest prophets nor the mightiest apostles nor any of the righteous saints of any of the ages—has ever been perfect, but we must become perfect to gain a celestial inheritance. As it is with being born again, and as it is with sanctifying our souls, so becoming perfect in Christ is a process. . . .

As members of the Church, if we chart a course leading to eternal life; if we begin the processes of spiritual rebirth, and are going in the right direction; if we chart a course of sanctifying our souls, and degree by degree are going in that direction; and if we chart a course of becoming perfect, and, step by step and phase by phase, are perfecting our souls by overcoming the world, then it is absolutely guaranteed—there is no question whatever about it—we shall gain eternal life. Even though we have spiritual rebirth ahead of us, perfection ahead of us, the full degree of sanctification ahead of us, if we chart a course and follow it to the best of our ability in this life, then when we go out of this life we'll continue in exactly that same course. We'll no longer be subject to the passions and the appetites of the flesh. We will have passed successfully the tests of this mortal probation and in due course we'll get the fulness of our Father's kingdom—and that means eternal life in his everlasting presence.

The Prophet told us that there are many things that people have to do, even after the grave, to work out their salvation. We're not going to be perfect the minute we die. But if we've charted a course, if our desires are right, if our appetites are curtailed and bridled, and if we believe in the Lord and are doing to the very best of our abilities what we ought to do, we'll go on to everlasting salvation, which is the fulness of eternal reward in our Father's kingdom.

Elder McConkie then observed: "I think we ought to have hope; I think we ought to have rejoicing."[7]

Few of those who have embraced the ways of the world will enter the gate and traverse the strait and narrow path. Many of our Father's children, however, even "an innumerable company" of the just (see D&C 76:67; 138:12), will come out of the world, get onto the path, and continue faithful until they fall down at the base of that tree whose fruit is the most desirable of all things and the most joyous to the soul.

The Promise of Salvation

The Lord has declared anew in our dispensation that "he who doeth the works of righteousness shall receive his reward, even peace in this world, and eternal life in the world to come" (D&C 59:23). Isaiah had written some twenty-six hundred years earlier, "And the work of righteousness shall be peace; and the effect of righteousness quietness and assurance for ever" (Isaiah 32:17). Those in this life who conduct themselves with fidelity and devotion to God and his laws shall eventually know that peace "which passeth all understanding" (Philippians 4:7), the calming but powerful assurance that one has successfully met the challenges of mortality. These are they who have lived by every word of God and are willing to serve the Lord at all hazards. They have made their callings and elections sure.[8] For them the day of judgment has been advanced, and the blessings associated with the glories of the celestial kingdom are assured. They receive what the Prophet Joseph called "the more sure word of prophecy." "The more sure word of prophecy," he explained, "means a man's knowing that he is sealed up unto eternal life, by revelation and the spirit of prophecy, through the power of the Holy Priesthood. It is impossible for a man to be saved in ignorance." (D&C 131:5–6.) Though it is true, as President Marion G. Romney observed, that "the fulness of eternal life is not attainable in mortality, . . . the peace which is its harbinger and which comes as a result of making one's calling and election sure is attainable in this life."[9]

The Prophet Joseph Smith extended the following challenging invitation to the Saints: "I would exhort you to go on and continue to call upon God until you make your calling and election sure for yourselves, by obtaining this more sure word of prophecy, and wait patiently for the promise until you obtain it."[10] Latter-day Saints who have received the ordinances of salvation—including the blessings of the temple endowment and eternal marriage—may thus press forward in the work of the Lord and with quiet dignity and patient maturity seek to be worthy of gaining the certain assurance of salvation before the end of their mortal lives. But should one not formally receive the more sure word of prophecy in this life, he has the scriptural promise that faithfully enduring to the end—keeping the covenants and commandments from baptism to the end of his life (see Mosiah 18:8–9)—eventuates in the promise of eternal life, whether that promise be received here or hereafter. (See D&C 14:7; 53:7; 2 Nephi 31:20; Mosiah 5:15.) "But *blessed are they who are faithful and endure, whether in life or in death, for they shall inherit eternal life"* (D&C 50:5; italics added). Bruce R. McConkie expressed the following sentiments at the funeral of Elder S. Dilworth Young:

> *If we die in the faith, that is the same thing as saying that our calling and election has been made sure and that we will go on to eternal reward hereafter.* As far as faithful members of the Church are concerned, they have charted a course leading to eternal life. This life is the time that is appointed as a probationary estate for men to prepare to meet God, and *as far as faithful people are concerned, if they are in the line of their duty, if they are doing what they ought to do, although they may not have been perfect in this sphere, their probation is ended. Now there will be some probation for some other people hereafter. But for the faithful saints of God, now is the time and the day, and their probation is ended with their death, and they will not thereafter depart from the path.* It is true as the Prophet Joseph Smith said, that there are many things that have to be done "even beyond the grave" to work out our salvation, but we'll stay in the course and we will not alter from it, if we have been true and faithful in this life.[11]

Conclusion

Salvation in the highest heaven is a reality and a possibility, a goal within the reach of all mankind. These precious promises—made available through the atoning blood of Jesus our Lord—give focus and direction to our actions.

Salvation, eternal life, eternal lives, exaltation—all expressions connoting the glories of the celestial kingdom and a life which is similar to God's own life—represent the grand ends to our myriad means, the reason we do what we do in the Church and in the home. To those who have developed "like precious faith" with the ancients come the blessings enjoyed by the ancients: the fulness of the glory of the Father and a continuation of the seeds forever and ever. We exult, "How glorious is the voice we hear from heaven, proclaiming in our ears, glory, and salvation, and honor, and immortality, and eternal life; kingdoms, principalities, and powers!" (D&C 128:23.)

11

From Everlasting
to Everlasting

Then shall they be gods, because they have no end; therefore shall they be from everlasting to everlasting, because they continue; then shall they be above all, because all things are subject unto them. Then shall they be gods, because they have all power, and the angels are subject unto them.

—D&C 132:20

The gospel has been restored, the heavens have been opened, the veil has been rent, and the great God, the Father of us all, has been revealed. The secret of the ages has been made known—God is an exalted man! We are in reality his children and thus of the lineage of the Gods. Our spirits were begotten of heavenly parents, our mortal bodies bear God's image and likeness, and our destiny is to become as he is. Let then the heavens ring with these singular truths: God is our Father! We are his children! We can become as he is. Let none in the household of faith be guilty of reducing these exalted verities to myth or metaphor, and let then our names be numbered in that book of remembrance, commenced by father Adam, in which a "genealogy was kept of the children of God" (Moses 6:8).

Eternity Past

Among the myriad truths revealed to the Prophet Joseph Smith as a part of the doctrinal restoration, perhaps none is more glorious and instructive than the simple reality of the premortal existence of man. It is a doctrine which is both logical and soul-expanding, a verity to which the Spirit of God can and will bear a powerful witness. Perhaps Joseph Smith's first encounter with this truth came in his work with the Book of Mormon, as he translated the thirteenth chapter of the book of Alma. It is here that the prophet Alma speaks of those who were "called and prepared from the foundation of the world" to receive the blessings of the priesthood, and of those who demonstrated "exceeding faith and good works" in that pristine existence, thereby qualifying for special opportunities in their second or mortal estate. We have no way of knowing how much light this one chapter shed forth upon the Saints during the early days of the Restoration; in fact, Elder Orson Pratt indicated that had additional and subsequent light and knowledge not been forthcoming in regard to this doctrine, he probably would not have recognized or discerned the mystery in Alma 13.[1]

It was while the Prophet was engaged in his inspired translation of the Bible that the mind of the latter-day seer was enlightened in regard to the matter of man's pre-earthly existence. While translating the book of Genesis, Joseph came to know of the Grand Council in Heaven, of the occasion wherein the Lord Jehovah was chosen as the chief advocate and proponent of the plan of the Eternal Father, and of the time when Lucifer and his hosts were cast from heaven and denied forever the opportunity for a second estate (see Moses 4:1–4). Additional details of this life before life were forthcoming as Joseph Smith translated the papyrus which came to be known as the book of Abraham. This Abrahamic account spoke of the time wherein the father of the faithful saw in vision the premortal spirits. Abraham's attention was directed to the "noble and great ones," of whom the Lord said, "These I will make my rulers" (Abraham 3:22–23). Through the lenses of modern revelation, Latter-day Saints were able to recognize—in heretofore mysterious biblical passages—allusions to the life before mortal birth. Answers were found to age-old questions, while meaning and purpose began to replace hopelessness and doubt. Elder Boyd K. Packer observed: "There is no way to make sense out of life without a knowledge of the doctrine of premortal life. The idea that mortal birth is the beginning is preposterous. There is no way to explain life if you believe that. The notion that life ends with mortal death is ridiculous. There is no way to face life if you believe that. When we understand the doctrine of premortal life, then things fit together and make sense."[2]

The revelations of the Restoration make plain the fact that "man was also in the beginning with God" (D&C 93:29). An official statement of the First Presidency issued in 1909 affirmed: "The doctrine of the pre-existence—revealed so plainly, particularly in latter days, pours a wonderful flood of light upon the otherwise mysterious problem of man's origin. It shows that *man, as a spirit, was begotten and born of heavenly parents, and reared to maturity in the eternal mansions of the Father, prior to coming upon the earth in a temporal body to undergo an experience in mortality.*"[3] Further, in speaking of the diverse nature of spirits that always follows as a result of free agency, Elder Bruce R. McConkie has written:

> Being subject to law, and having their agency, all the spirits of men, while yet in the Eternal Presence, developed aptitudes, talents, capacities, and abilities of every sort, kind, and degree. During the long expanse of life which then was, an infinite variety of talents and abilities came into being. As the ages rolled, no two spirits remained alike. Mozart became a musician; Einstein centered his interest in mathematics; Michelangelo turned his attention to painting. Cain was a liar, a schemer, a rebel who maintained a close affinity with Lucifer. Abraham and Moses and all of the prophets sought and obtained the talent for spirituality. Mary and Eve were two of the greatest of all the spirit daughters of the father. The whole

house of Israel, known and segregated out from their fellows, was inclined toward spiritual things. And so it went through all the hosts of heaven, each individual developing such talents and abilities as his soul desired.[4]

And thus we see that diversity and difference are not qualities descriptive only of the mortal and postmortal realms; from the period of time prior to mortal birth, man has chosen to distinguish himself (one way or the other) by his actions. President Harold B. Lee taught:

> May I ask each of you again the question, "Who are you?" You are all the sons and daughters of God. Your spirits were created and lived as organized intelligences before the world was. You have been blessed to have a physical body because of your obedience to certain commandments in that premortal state. You are now born into a family to which you have come, into the nations through which you have come, as a reward for the kind of lives you lived before you came here and at a time in the world's history, as the Apostle Paul taught the men of Athens [Acts 17:24–27] and as the Lord revealed to Moses [Deuteronomy 32:8–9], determined by the faithfulness of each of those who lived before this world was created. . . .
>
> It would seem very clear, then [having just quoted Paul and Moses], that those born to the lineage of Jacob . . . were born into the most illustrious lineage of any of those who came upon the earth as mortal beings.
>
> All these rewards were seemingly promised, or foreordained, before the world was. Surely these matters must have been determined by the kind of lives we had lived in that premortal spirit world. Some may question these assumptions, but at the same time they will accept without any question the belief that each one of us will be judged when we leave this earth according to his deeds during our lives here in mortality. Isn't it just as reasonable to believe that what we have received here in this earth life was given to each of us according to the merits of our conduct before we came here?[5]

Life—for man and God—is a grand continuum, extending from one aspect of eternity, then into time, then back into eternity.

As God Once Was

"There are but a very few beings in the world," Joseph Smith stated in the King Follett Sermon, "who understand rightly the character of God. The great majority of mankind do not comprehend anything, either that which is past, or that which is to come, as it respects their relationship to God. They do not know, neither do they understand the nature of that relationship; and consequently they know but little above the brute beast, or more than to eat, drink, and sleep. This is all man knows about God or his existence, unless it is given by the inspiration of the Almighty."[6] The choice seer of the Restoration then tore away the cobwebs of the past, rent the veil of unbelief and ignorance, and shattered the religious traditions of the day regarding the Great God who dwells in heaven. He taught of God's past, which thereby unfolded man's future and potential destiny. Comparing the natures of God and man, the Prophet said: *"If men do not comprehend the character of God, they do not comprehend themselves."*[7] "I will go back to the beginning before the world was, to show what kind of being God is. What sort of a being was God in the beginning?" Joseph then invited the Saints to gaze with him upon the scenes of eternity:

> God himself was once as we are now, and is an exalted man, and sits enthroned in yonder heavens! That is the great secret. If the veil were rent today, and the great God who holds this world in its orbit, and who upholds all worlds and all things by his power, was to make himself visible,—I say, if you were to see him today, you would see him like a man in form—like yourselves in all the person, image, and very form as a man; for Adam was created in the very fashion, image and likeness of God, and received instruction from, and walked, talked and conversed with him, as one man talks and communes with another.
>
> In order to understand the subject of the dead, for consolation of those who mourn for the loss of their friends [note how the Prophet here ties an understanding of God's true

nature to a deeper peace associated with life after death], it is necessary we should understand the character and being of God and how he came to be so; for I am going to tell you how God came to be God. We have imagined and supposed that God was God from all eternity. I will refute that idea, and take away the veil, so that you may see.

These are incomprehensible ideas to some, but they are simple. It is the first principle of the Gospel to know for a certainty the Character of God, and to know that we may converse with him as one man converses with another, and that he was once a man like us; yea, that God himself, the Father of us all, dwelt on an earth, the same as Jesus Christ himself did. . . . [8]

Expanding upon that which he had learned from the Prophet Joseph, Brigham Young explained that God the Father "has passed the ordeals we are now passing through; he has received an experience, has suffered and enjoyed, and knows all that we know regarding the toils, sufferings, life and death of this mortality, for he has passed through the whole of it, and has received his crown and exaltation."[9]

How much more perfect and complete can our worship of the Great God be when we come to know of his true character! How appropriate it is for mortal man to worship and give total devotion and allegiance to an exalted Man, a Man of Holiness. To know that eons ago our God was once a man does not lessen him in our esteem or perspective, but rather opens the divine door to an infinitude of possibilities regarding man. President Brigham Young observed, "Some believe or conceive the idea that to know God would lessen him in our estimation; but I can say that for me to understand any principle or being, on earth or in Heaven, it does not lessen its true value to me, but, on the contrary, it increases it; and the more I can know of God, the dearer and more precious He is to me, and the more exalted are my feelings toward Him."[10]

As God Now Is

Our Father's development and progression over an infinitely long period of time has brought him to the point at

which he now presides as God Almighty, He who is omni-
potent, omniscient, and, by means of his Holy Spirit, omnipresent: he has all power, all knowledge, and is, through the
Light of Christ, in and through all things. In speaking of the
importance of our God possessing all knowledge in order
for his children to exercise faith in him, Joseph Smith
explained, "Without the knowledge of <u>all things</u> God would
not be able to save any portion of his creatures; for it is by
reason of the knowledge which he has of all things, from the
beginning to the end, that enables him to give that understanding to his creatures by which they are made partakers
of eternal life; and if it were not for the idea existing in the
minds of men that God had all knowledge it would be
impossible for them to exercise faith in him."[11] Joseph Smith
went on to teach those in the School of the Prophets that
what was true of God's knowledge was true of every other
virtue: the Father of us all possesses all principles and all
attributes (for example, faith or power, justice, judgment,
mercy, and truth) in perfection.[12] Elder Bruce R. McConkie
has commented as follows in regard to God's perfections:

> In other words, where every attribute and every character-
> istic are concerned, the Lord is perfect and in him is embodied
> the totality of what is involved. Can anyone suppose that God
> does not have all charity, that he falls short in integrity or
> honesty, or that there is any truth that he does not know?
> There is a statement in our literature that says that the Prophet
> and his associates learned, by translating the papyrus received
> from the catacombs of Egypt, that life had been going on in
> this system for <u>2,555,000,000 years</u>. It seems reasonable to me
> that a God who has been creating, expanding, governing, and
> regulating worlds for a period that is so infinite that you and I
> have no way of comprehending its duration has attained a
> state where he knows all things and nothing is withheld.[13]

Our God progresses in the sense that his kingdoms
expand and his dominions multiply. As his children participate in the new and everlasting covenant of marriage and
thereafter prove worthy of the blessings associated with that
order of priesthood, then "by this law is the continuation of
the works of my Father, *wherein he glorifieth himself*"

(D&C 132:32; italics added; cf. v. 63). Joseph Smith, speaking for the Savior in the King Follett Sermon, said: "My Father worked out his kingdom with fear and trembling, and I must do the same; and when I get my kingdom, I shall present it to my Father, so that he may obtain kingdom upon kingdom, and it will exalt him in glory. He will then take a higher exaltation, and I will take his place, and thereby become exalted myself." The Prophet then continued: "So that Jesus treads in the tracks of his Father, and inherits what God did before; and *God is thus glorified and exalted in the salvation and exaltation of all his children.*"[14]

What Man May Become

As early as February of 1832, in the Vision of the Glories, Joseph Smith learned by revelation of a righteous man's possibilities beyond the grave. In speaking of those who come forth in the resurrection of the just with a celestial body, the revelation stated: "They are they who are the church of the Firstborn. They are they into whose hands the Father has given all things—they are they who are priests and kings, who have received of his fulness, and of his glory; and are priests of the Most High, after the order of Melchizedek, which was after the order of Enoch, which was after the order of the Only Begotten Son. Wherefore, as it is written, *they are gods, even the sons of God.*" (D&C 76:54–58; italics added.) In the *Lectures on Faith* Joseph taught further that "all those who keep his [God's] commandments shall grow up from grace to grace, and become heirs of the heavenly kingdom, and joint heirs with Jesus Christ; possessing the same mind, being transformed into the same image or likeness, even the express image of him who fills all in all; being filled with the fullness of his glory, and become one in him, even as the Father, Son, and Holy Spirit are one."[15]

While attending a patriarchal blessing meeting in 1836, young Lorenzo Snow was told by Joseph Smith Sr., "You will become as great as you can possibly wish—even as great as God, and you cannot wish to be greater."[16] In the spring of 1840 Elder Lorenzo Snow had a singular spiritual experience. He writes: "The Spirit of the Lord rested mightily upon me—the eyes of my understanding were opened, and I saw as clear as the sun at noonday, with wonder and astonishment, the pathway of God and man. I formed the following couplet which expresses the revelation, as it was shown me, and explains Father Smith's dark saying to me at a blessing meeting in the Kirtland Temple, prior to my baptism." The couplet was recorded as follows: "As man now is, God once was; As God now is, man may be." After the Prophet Joseph Smith's Follett Sermon, Lorenzo felt he could then teach the doctrine publicly.[17] The couplet is expanded in the following poem penned by Brother Snow in response to the Apostle John's statement in 1 John 3:1–3:

Dear Brother:

> Hast thou not been unwisely bold,
> Man's destiny to thus unfold?
> To raise, promote such high desire,
> Such vast ambition thus inspire?

> Still, 'tis no phantom that we trace
> Man's ultimatum in life's race;
> This royal path has long been trod
> By righteous men, each now a God:

> As Abra'm, Isaac, Jacob, too,
> First babes, then men—to gods they grew.
> As man now is, our God once was;
> As now God is, so man may be—
> Which doth unfold man's destiny.

> For John declares: When Christ we see
> Like unto him we'll truly be.
> And he who has this hope within,
> Will purify himself from sin.

> Who keep this object grand in view,
> To folly, sin, will bid adieu,
> Nor wallow in the mire anew;

Nor ever seek to carve his name
High on the shaft of worldly fame;
But here his ultimatum trace:
The head of all his spirit race.

Ah, well: that taught by you, dear Paul,
'Though much amazed, we see it all;
Our Father God, has ope'ed our eyes,
We cannot view it otherwise.

The boy, like to his father grown,
Has but attained unto his own;
To grow to sire from state of son,
Is not 'gainst Nature's course to run.

A son of God, like God to be,
Would not be robbing Deity;
And he who has this hope within,
Will purify himself from sin.

You're right, St. John, supremely right:
Whoe'er essays to climb this height,
Will cleanse himself from sin entire—
Or else 'twere needless to aspire.[18]

Who is there among mortal men that can fully grasp these transcendent verities? Man may become as God himself! Let those who disagree howl as they may! Such is within the reach of all who will pay the price. This marvelous accomplishment—the ability to be even as our exalted Sire—is the consummation of that process of spiritual development which begins in premortality, continues with an accelerated pace while in the flesh, and moves on to realization in the worlds beyond the grave. Joseph Smith the Prophet thus gave the supreme definition of eternal life: "Here, then, is eternal life—to know the only wise and true God; and you have got to learn how to be Gods yourselves, and to be kings and priests to God, the same as all Gods have done before you, namely, by going from one small degree to another, and from a small capacity to a great one; from grace to grace, from exaltation to exaltation, until you attain to the resurrection of the dead, and are able to dwell in everlasting burnings, and to sit in glory, as do those who sit enthroned in everlasting power."[19]

Conclusion

By opening the veil and revealing the nature and kind of being God is, Joseph the Prophet thereby made known in concurrent fashion what the nature and kind of being man is. Man is of the same species as God, and as such has the capacity, through extended righteousness and faith, to rise to the station of a god. Our God is not possessive of godhood, but is an exalted Father who pleads with his posterity with tender regard to follow the path he has already trod, a path which leads not only to the ultimate in joy and happiness, but also to a complete realization of all it was intended for man to become. The cup with its draught of possibilities beyond the grave runneth over, a cup extended to the obedient. The beckoning call of the Lord is, "Drink, then, the heavenly draught, and live!"

12

That All May Be Saved

Now the great and grand secret of the whole matter, and the summum bonum of the whole subject that is lying before us, consists in obtaining the powers of the Holy Priesthood. For him to whom these keys are given there is no difficulty in obtaining a knowledge of facts in relation to the salvation of the children of men, both as well for the dead as for the living.

—D&C 128:11

It is for God to ordain that system by which the veil is to be rent and mortals permitted to see and know of future glories. It is for him to call prophets, bequeath priesthood, give keys, and reveal the plan of salvation. This he has done. Let the message be heralded! "Hear, O ye heavens, and give ear, O earth, and rejoice ye inhabitants thereof" (D&C 76:1). "Let all the nations be gathered together, and let the people be assembled: who among them can declare this, and shew us former things? let them bring forth their witnesses, that they may be justified: or let them hear, and say, It is truth" (Isaiah 43:9).

The Restoration of All Things

All the holy prophets since the world began have heralded a final day in which all things are to be restored, in which all things are to be gathered in one (see Acts 3:21; Ephesians 1:10). Such is the dispensation of which we are a part, the dispensation of the fulness of all past dispensations, "which dispensation is now beginning to usher in, that a whole and complete and perfect union, and welding together of dispensations, and keys, and powers, and glories should take place, and be revealed from the days of Adam even to the present time. And not only this, but those things which never have been revealed from the foundation of the world, but have been kept hid from the wise and prudent, shall be revealed unto babes and sucklings in this, the dispensation of the fulness of times." (D&C 128:18.)

To those who first held the priesthood in this dispensation the Lord said: "Ye are lawful heirs, according to the flesh, and have been hid from the world with Christ in God —therefore your life and the priesthood have remained, and must needs remain through you and your lineage until the restoration of all things spoken by the mouths of all the holy prophets since the world began. Therefore, blessed are ye if ye continue in my goodness, a light unto the Gentiles, and through this priesthood, a savior unto my people Israel." (D&C 86:9–11.) Regarding the restoration of the keys of the priesthood the Lord said, "I have conferred upon you the keys and power of the priesthood, wherein I restore all things, and make known unto you all things in due time" (D&C 132:45). And then, speaking more specifically about the keys, knowledge, and authority necessary to labor for and in behalf of the dead, the Lord said, "For him to whom these keys are given there is no difficulty in obtaining a knowledge of facts in relation to the salvation of the children of men, both as well for the dead as for the living" (D&C 128:11).

Truths Known to the Ancients

Bible References to Vicarious Ordinances

The knowledge that the gospel was to be taught to all, either in this life or the next, and that vicarious ordinances were to be performed for those unable to receive them in earth life, was known to the ancient Saints. There are scriptural, apocryphal, and historical references that evidence that these principles were understood anciently. Yet it is only with the knowledge we have as a result of the restoration of the gospel that these ancient sources take on significant meaning for us; otherwise they would seem as strange to Latter-day Saints as they presently do to the rest of the Christian world. One revelation unfolds another, the present unfolds the past, and the past unfolds the present. Isaiah wrote, "And they shall be gathered together, as prisoners are gathered in the pit, and shall be shut up in the prison, and after many days shall they be visited" (Isaiah 24:22). Later he added that Christ would "proclaim liberty to the captives," and open "the prison to them that are bound" (Isaiah 61:1). Now note how perfectly the Vision of the Redemption of the Dead explains what Isaiah has written. The vision begins with Joseph F. Smith's description of paradise at the time of Christ's visit among the righteous, saying: "There were gathered together in one place an innumerable company of the spirits of the just, who had been faithful in the testimony of Jesus while they lived in mortality; and who had offered sacrifice in the similitude of the great sacrifice of the Son of God, and had suffered tribulation in their Redeemer's name. All these had departed the mortal life, firm in the hope of a glorious resurrection, through the grace of God the Father and his Only Begotten Son, Jesus Christ." Then President Smith said: "I beheld that they were filled with joy and gladness, and were rejoicing together because the day of their deliverance was at hand. They were assembled awaiting the advent of the Son of God into the spirit world, to declare their redemption from the bands of death." (D&C 138:12–16.) All the wisdom and commentary the world can provide cannot match a revelation from heaven.

A second example is found in this prophetic statement by Zechariah: "By the blood of thy covenant [that is, because of the gospel covenant, which is efficacious because of the shedding of the blood of Christ] I have sent forth thy prisoners out of *the pit wherein is no water*" (Zechariah 9:11; italics added). The pit is the spirit world, but what waters are necessary to free one from that captivity? Why, the waters of vicarious baptism—a doctrine taught by Paul and restored through the Prophet Joseph Smith. Paul asked, "Else what shall they do which are baptized for the dead, if the dead rise not at all? why are they then baptized for the dead?" (1 Corinthians 15:29). And Joseph Smith, in restoring the ordinances in our day, told us the baptismal font must be "in a place underneath where the living are wont to assemble, to show forth the living and the dead, and that all things may have their likeness, and that they may accord one with another—that which is earthly conforming to that which is heavenly" (D&C 128:13). As a third example, what of Malachi's prophecy of the return of Elijah to turn the hearts of the dead to their children in the flesh? Had Elijah not actually returned we would not know that the old prophet had "his eye fixed on the restoration of the priesthood" (D&C 128:17) and its sealing powers.

The world is hard pressed to give any meaningful explanation as to what took place during the forty days that Christ ministered to the Twelve following his resurrection (see Acts 1:3). In fact, their attempts at commentary are embarrassingly poor.[1] To Latter-day Saints the matter seems most obvious. What would be more natural than to expect his Apostles to ask about his experiences in death and for him to respond? In so doing he would tell of those things described for us in the Vision of the Redemption of the Dead (D&C 138); that is, he would tell of his visit to paradise where he met with the "innumerable company of the spirits of the just" who had faithfully lived the gospel while in the flesh. He would report to the Apostles about having organized a mission in the spirit world and having called various of the prophets and faithful of dispensations past to teach the gospel to those in darkness. That is, he turned the key, or gave his commission for missionary work to commence among those in the bondage of sin and ignorance. Having so explained, it is most natural to suppose that his disciples would ask how the gospel message would differ in the spirit realm. They would be told, as we are in Joseph F. Smith's great vision, that an everlasting gospel does not change (see D&C 138:11–35). Such a response would then raise questions about how gospel ordinances—for instance, the ordinance of baptism—were to be performed among them that were dead. Thus the stage was set for the major purpose of the forty-day ministry—to teach the nature of vicarious ordinances, and to instruct the Apostles in the fulness of the temple ceremony.

Historical References to the Teaching of the Gospel to the Dead

Hosea prophesied that the Messiah would ransom men from "the power of the grave" and that he would "redeem them from death" (Hosea 13:14). Rabbinic commentary on this verse held that those who were bound in Gehinnom would rejoice at the appearance of the Messiah, "saying, He will lead us forth from this darkness."[2] According to the *Zohar,* a collection of Jewish mysticism, the righteous, or the patriarchs, descended to hell to rescue sinners from the place of torment. The influence of Talmudic doctrines is also found in the old Islamic theology where it is held that the righteous "who have safely passed the bridge which crosses Hell to Paradise, intercede for their brethren detained upon it. They are sent to Hell to see if any there have faith, and to bring them out. These are washed in the Water of Life and admitted to Paradise."[3]

"The Talmud teaches that the offerings and prayers made by the living for the dead shorten their stay in Gehenna."[4] The apocryphal book of 2 Maccabees recounts a story in which Judas, a Maccabean general, took up a collection for Jewish soldiers fallen in battle that was sent to Jerusalem to pay for a sin offering in their behalf. The text reads: "Therefore he made atonement for the dead, that they might be delivered from their sin."[5] Though we would hold this to be bad doctrine, we are left to wonder at the origin of the idea of ordinances for and in behalf of the dead.

The idea of continuous gospel study beyond the grave was very much a part of Jewish tradition. Frequent reference is made in the Haggadah to the "heavenly academy" in which the pious dead study the Law.[6] It was also held that the revelations of God were given for the benefit of both the living and the dead. For instance, when Jehovah spoke at Sinai, "the revelation took place in the presence of the living as well as of the dead, yea, even the souls of those who were not yet born were present."[7]

There is evidence that such knowledge, long lost to the Christian world, was once known to them. Early Christian commentary on the statement in Hebrews that "they without us should not be made perfect" (Hebrews 11:40) held that it had reference to the Old Testament Saints who were trapped in Hades awaiting the help of their New Testament counterparts and that Christ held the keys that would "open the doors of the Underworld to the faithful souls there."[8]

"About the middle of the second century Justin Martyr, in his *Dialogue with Trypho* (c. 72), cites an apocryphon which he charges the Jews with having deleted from the Book of Jeremiah, though it was still to be found in some synagogue copies: 'And the Lord God of Israel remembered His dead ones, who sleep in the earth of dust, and He descended to preach to them His salvation.'"[9] "In his commentary on S. Luke, Origen expounds further this conception of the way to the tree of life in Paradise. There is a fiery river through which all must pass, receiving a baptism of fire. It cannot harm the righteous, but all who are baptized with water and the Spirit, receive that fiery baptism and so pass to Paradise. To this Paradise *in terra,* better than Hades, but not the heavenly Paradise, and guarded by the cherubim with the fiery sword, our Lord transferred those whom He rescued from Hades."[10]

Irenaeus, bishop of Lyons in France during the latter quarter of the second century, reasoned that it was not merely for those who lived during the time of Tiberius Caesar that Christ came, "nor did the Father exercise His providence for the men only who are now alive, but for all men altogether, who from the beginning, according to their capacity, in their generation have both feared and loved God, and practiced justice and piety towards their neighbors, and have earnestly desired to see Christ, and to hear His voice." All these, Irenaeus argued, were to come forth in an early resurrection and be given place in the kingdom of heaven. Each, he held, would receive "recompense for those things which they accomplished."[11]

Clement, called "the founder of Christian literature," and contemporary of Irenaeus, wrote with even greater clarity on the matter. The sixth chapter of his work *Miscellanies,* bears the title, "The Gospel Was Preached To Jews And Gentiles In Hades." In this chapter he not only announces that Christ taught the gospel in the world of spirits but that his Apostles did likewise. "For, it was requisite," he reasoned, "that as here, so also there, the best of the disciples should be imitators of the Master." Clement held that it was necessary to teach the gospel to the departed spirits because they could not be saved in ignorance.

As to the issue of whether Christ taught all that were in the spirit world or only the Jews, Clement reasoned as follows:

> If, then, the Lord descended to Hades for no other end but to preach the gospel, as He did descend; it was either to preach the gospel to all or to the Hebrews only. If, accordingly, to all, then all who believe shall be saved, although they may be of the Gentiles, on making their profession there; since God's punishments are saving and disciplinary, leading to conversion, and choosing rather the repentance than the death of a sinner; and especially since souls, although darkened by passions, when released from their bodies, are able to perceive more clearly, because of their being no longer obstructed by the paltry flesh.
>
> If, then, He preached only to the Jews, who wanted the knowledge and faith of the Saviour, it is plain that, since God

is no respecter of persons, the apostles also, as here, so there, preached the gospel to those of the heathen who were ready for conversion. [12]

Clement held that those "who were outside the Law" in mortality but who lived rightly would, "on hearing the voice of the Lord, whether that of His own person or that acting through His apostles," with "all speed" turn to the gospel and believe. "So I think it is demonstrated," he said, "that God being good, and the Lord powerful, they save with a righteousness and equality which extend to all that turn to Him, whether here or elsewhere."[13]

A dispensation of the gospel on earth required a dispensation of the gospel in the spirit world, according to Clement. He wrote as follows:

> Did not the same dispensation obtain in Hades, so that even there, all the souls, on hearing the proclamation, might either exhibit repentance, or confess that their punishment was just, because they believed not? And it were the exercise of no ordinary arbitrariness, for those who had departed before the advent of the Lord (not having the gospel preached to them, and having afforded no ground from themselves, in consequence of believing or not) to obtain either salvation or punishment. For it is not right that these should be condemned without trial, and that those alone who lived after the advent should have the advantage of "Whatever one of you has done in ignorance, without clearly knowing God if, on becoming conscious, he repent, all his sins will be forgiven him."[14]

Clement reasoned that if Christ "preached the gospel to those in the flesh that they might not be condemned unjustly, how is it conceivable that He did not for the same cause preach the gospel to those who had departed this life before His advent?"[15] There were three principles that were common to the writings of the Apostolic Fathers as they wrote about Christ's descent to Hades to redeem the dead: first, that as Christ had forerunners to announce his coming on earth so he had forerunners to announce his coming in the world of the spirits. For instance, Hippolytus held that

John the Baptist went to prepare the way for the Lord in the spirit realm. Origen agreed but also maintained that Moses and the other Old Testament prophets were already testifying to the spirits that Christ would come. The Fathers also held that the Apostles and faithful from Christ's dispensation would continue their preaching in the spirit world, and finally that baptism was "absolutely necessary" to the salvation of the dead. Little mention is given to the idea of vicarious baptism (see 1 Corinthians 15:29); rather, it was most generally held that those baptisms were performed in Hades.[16]

The Descent in Apocryphal Writings

In Christian apocryphal writings the visit of Christ to the spirits in prison held a prominent place. For instance, in the *Odes of Solomon*, we may have the earliest writings on this subject outside of the New Testament. Ode 17:6–17 reads as follows:

And all who saw me were amazed,
and I seemed to them like a stranger.

And he who knew and exalted me
is the Most High in all his perfection.

And he glorified me by his kindness,
and raised my understanding to the height of truth.

And from there he gave me the way of his paths,
and I opened the doors which were closed.

And I shattered the bars of iron, for my
own iron(s) had grown hot and melted before me.

And nothing appeared close to me
because I was the opening of everything.

And I went toward all my bondsmen in order to loose them; that I might not abandon anyone bound or binding.

And I gave my knowledge generously,
and my resurrection through my love.

And I sowed my fruits in hearts,
and transformed them through myself.

Then they received my blessing and lived,
and they were gathered to me and were saved;

Because they became my members,
and I was their head.[17]

Other Odes speak of Christ being given "authority over chains" so that he might "loose them" (Ode 22:4), of his opening and closing the chasms of the dead (Ode 24:5), and of death ejecting him with many others (Ode 42:11). From Ode 42:14–20 we read the following:

And I made a congregation of living among his dead;
and I spoke with them by living lips;
in order that my word may not fail.

And those who had died ran toward me; and
they cried out and said, "Son of God, have pity on us.

"And deal with us according to your kindness,
and bring us out from the chains of darkness.

"And open for us the door
by which we may go forth to you,
for we perceive that our death does not approach you.

"May we also be saved with you,
because you are our Savior."

Then I heard their voice,
and placed their faith in my heart.

And I placed my name upon their head,
because they are free and they are mine.[18]

From the *Epistle of the Apostles,* a work believed to have originated about A.D. 160 in Asia Minor, Christ is quoted as saying: "I descended to the place of Lazarus and preached to the righteous and the prophets, that they might come out of the rest which is below, and go up to that which is above. And I poured out over them with my right hand (the water) of life and forgiveness and deliverance from all evil, as I have done to you and to those who believe in Me."[19]

Conclusion

Everything that the Lord does and says carries with it the evidence of its own authenticity, and every child of God has been divinely endowed with the ability to recognize and know these truths. We know of no greater evidence that the gospel has been restored in these the latter days than the light that surrounds the revelations of the Restoration. They evidence themselves, and nowhere is this more evident than in those revelations that part the veil and allow us to see beyond the grave. The combined intellect and wisdom of all the world cannot begin to match the majesty and power of such revelations as the Vision of the Glories (D&C 76), the Vision of the Celestial Kingdom (D&C 137), and the Vision of the Redemption of the Dead (D&C 138). Such divine light exalts the souls of men.

The words of these sublime revelations are fashioned in the image and likeness of their maker; in mercy, grace, and justice they resemble the God from whence they came. James told us that "the wisdom that is from above is first pure, then peaceable, gentle, and easy to be intreated, full of mercy and good fruits, without partiality, and without hypocrisy" (James 3:17). "That which is of God is light" (D&C 50:24), it lifts and ennobles, it brings peace and consolation, it enhances faith and fires the soul, it brings men worthily to God. These revelations constitute what might be called the law of the mourner, by which we "weep for the loss of them that die, and more especially for those that have not hope of a glorious resurrection" (D&C 42:45), while for those of the household of faith our tears are tears of rejoicing, for we know the glories that await us.

Notes

Chapter 1. Parting the Veil

1. *Juvenile Instructor,* vol. 27 (15 May 1892), pp. 303–4.

2. *History of The Church of Jesus Christ of Latter-day Saints,* 7 vols., ed. B. H. Roberts (Salt Lake City: Deseret Book Co., 1957), 1:252–53; italics added.

3. Milton V. Backman Jr., *The Heavens Resound: A History of the Latter-day Saints in Ohio, 1830–1838* (Salt Lake City: Deseret Book Co., 1983), p. 285.

4. *History of the Church,* 2:379–80.

5. See Bruce R. McConkie, "The Doctrinal Restoration," in *The Joseph Smith Translation: The Restoration of Plain and Precious Things,* ed. Monte S. Nyman and Robert L. Millet (Provo, Utah: Religious Studies Center, Brigham Young University, 1985), pp. 1–22.

6. Donald Q. Cannon and Larry E. Dahl, *The Prophet Joseph Smith's King Follett Discourse: A Six-Column Comparison of Original Notes and Amalgamations* (Provo, Utah: Religious Studies Center, Brigham Young University, 1983), pp. 1–2.

7. Mary C. Westover, *Young Woman's Journal,* XVII (December 1906), p. 545.

8. *Teachings of the Prophet Joseph Smith,* comp. Joseph Fielding Smith (Salt Lake City: Deseret Book Co., 1976), p. 345.

9. Joseph F. Smith, Conference Report, October 1918, p 2; italics added.

10. Joseph Fielding Smith, *The Life of Joseph F. Smith* (Salt Lake City: Deseret Book Co., 1969), p. 455.

11. Ibid., p. 474.

12. *Journal of Discourses,* 26 vols. (Liverpool: F. D. Richards & Sons, 1855–86), 9:288; italics added.

Chapter 2. The World of Spirits

1. Bruce R. McConkie, Conference Report, October 1976, p. 157.

2. *Diary of Charles Lowell Walker,* 2 vols., ed. A. Karl and Katherine Miles Larsen (Logan, Utah: Utah State University Press, 1980), 1:465–66; italics added.

3. *Journal of Discourses,* 1:7.

4. *Teachings of the Prophet Joseph Smith,* p. 326; italics added.

5. Parley P. Pratt, *Key to the Science of Theology,* 9th ed. (Salt Lake City: Deseret Book Co., 1965), pp. 126–27; italics added; see also Brigham Young, *Journal of Discourses,* 3:367–69.

6. *Journal of Discourses,* 3:368.

7. Orson Pratt, ibid., 16:365.

8. *Gospel Truth,* 2 vols., comp. Jerreld L. Newquist (Salt Lake City: Zion's Book Store, 1957), 1:73.

9. *Journal of Discourses,* 3:112–13.

10. Ibid., 3:369.

11. Ibid., 2:150; cf. Parley P. Pratt, *Key to the Science of Theology,* pp. 127–28.

12. Joseph F. Smith, *Gospel Doctrine* (Salt Lake City: Deseret Book Co., 1977), p. 448.

13. See Bruce R. McConkie, "A New Commandment: Save Thyself and Thy Kindred," *Ensign,* August 1976, p. 11.

14. *Journal of Discourses,* 1:289–90.

15. Ibid., 3:95; italics added.

16. There are some occasions wherein the word *hell* is used to refer to the spirit world. As we shall see later, *hell* is usually the word which describes that portion of the spirit world where sorrow and suffering and repentance are the order of things for the wicked who inhabit it. Note, however, the use of the word *hell* in Peter's sermon on Christ's soul not being left in hell (Acts 2:27, quoting Psalm 16:10). Appropriately, the Joseph Smith Translation of the verse in Acts renders the word *hell* as "prison."

17. *Teachings of the Prophet Joseph Smith,* p. 309; italics added. Josiah Quincy visited the Prophet Joseph Smith in Nauvoo and wrote later of an occasion wherein Joseph spoke on the necessity of baptism for salvation. A minister in the audience contended as follows with the Prophet: *"Minister.* Stop! What do you say to the case of the penitent thief? *Prophet.* What do you mean by that? *Minister.* You know our Saviour said to the thief, 'This day shalt thou be with me in Paradise,' which shows he could not have been baptized before his admission. *Prophet.* How do you know he wasn't baptized before he became a thief? At this retort the sort of laugh that is provoked by an unexpected hit ran through the audience; but this demonstration of sympathy was rebuked by a severe look from Smith, who went on to say: 'But that is not the true answer. In the original Greek, as this gentleman [turning to me] will inform you, the word that has been translated paradise means simply a place of departed spirits. To that place the penitent thief was conveyed, and there, doubtless, he received the baptism necessary for his admission to the heavenly kingdom.'" (*Figures of the Past* [Boston: Roberts Brothers, 1883], pp. 391–92.)

18. *Teachings of the Prophet Joseph Smith,* p. 310; italics added. Note also these words from Joseph Smith: "The righteous and the wicked all go to the same world of spirits until the resurrection." (Ibid.)

19. *Journal of Discourses,* 1:9.

20. With but few exceptions, *outer darkness* refers to hell, the place of suffering and sadness and confrontation in the spirit world. (See Alma 34:33; 40:13–14; 41:7; D&C 38:5; 138:22, 30, 57; Isaiah 49:9.)

21. *Teachings of the Prophet Joseph Smith,* pp. 310–11.

22. Ibid., p. 357.

23. For a discussion of how a large segment of modern Christianity has rejected the notions of Satan and hell, see Joseph Fielding McConkie, *Gospel Symbolism* (Salt Lake City: Bookcraft, 1985), pp. 210–11.

24. From "The Three Degrees of Glory," in *Melvin J. Ballard— Crusader for Righteousness* (Salt Lake City: Bookcraft, 1966), pp. 212–13; italics added.

25. *Journal of Discourses,* 1:11.

26. Bruce R. McConkie, *The Mortal Messiah,* 4 books (Salt Lake City: Deseret Book Co., 1979–81), 3:263; italics added.

27. See Joseph Fielding Smith, *The Way to Perfection* (Salt Lake City: Deseret Book Co., 1970), pp. 315–21.

28. *Teachings of the Prophet Joseph Smith,* p. 170; see also pp. 171, 191; D&C 7; 3 Nephi 28.

29. From Bruce R. McConkie, "Jesus Christ and Him Crucified," *1976 Brigham Young University Devotional Speeches of the Year* (Provo, Utah: Brigham Young University Press, 1977), p. 401; see also *The Millennial Messiah* (Salt Lake City: Deseret Book Co., 1982), pp. 284–85. Cf. D&C 138:57.

30. *Teachings of the Prophet Joseph Smith,* p. 359.

31. *Liahona—The Elders Journal,* 6:178 (27 October 1907).

Chapter 3. That All Might Hear

1. *Lectures on Faith* (Salt Lake City: Deseret Book Co., 1985), 7:9; italics added.

2. Bruce R. McConkie, "A New Commandment," *Ensign,* August 1976, p. 9.

3. Bruce R. McConkie, "All Are Alike unto God," Annual Religious Educators' Symposium (Salt Lake City: The Church of Jesus Christ of Latter-day Saints, 1978), p. 4.

4. From the account of Oliver Cowdery, it appears that the translators had reached the book of 3 Nephi when they determined to inquire of the Lord concerning baptism (*Messenger and Advocate,* vol. 1 [October, 1834], pp. 14–16).

5. *Times and Seasons* (February 1, 1843), 4:84.

6. See an interview with William Smith by E. C. Briggs and J. W. Peterson, published in the *Deseret News* (Salt Lake City), 20 January 1894.

7. Lucy Smith, *History of Joseph Smith by His Mother* (Salt Lake City: Bookcraft, 1958), p. 87.

8. Ibid., p. 89.

9. *History of the Church,* 5:126–27.

Chapter 4. The Gospel: Here and Hereafter

1. *Teachings of the Prophet Joseph Smith,* p. 158.

2. *Journal of Discourses,* 1:11.

3. *Gospel Doctrine,* pp. 471–72.

4. Ibid.

5. Examples of this principle will be given in chapter 6.

6. *Gospel Doctrine,* p. 461.

7. *Melvin J. Ballard . . . Crusader for Righteousness,* p. 217.

Chapter 5. Spirits: Their Knowledge and Power

1. Bruce R. McConkie, *Doctrinal New Testament Commentary,* 3 vols. (Salt Lake City: Bookcraft, 1973), 3:533.

2. Wilford Woodruff, *Deseret Weekly News,* 53:642–43.

3. *Journal of Discourses,* 1:10–11.

4. Ibid., p. 11.

5. Ibid., p. 12.

6. Ibid.

7. Ibid., p. 14.

Chapter 6. Angels: Our Companions

1. *Gospel Doctrine,* pp. 435–37.

2. Joseph Fielding McConkie, *His Name Shall Be Joseph* (Salt Lake City: Hawkes Publishing Co., 1980), p. 213.

3. This interpretation of the "keys of the ministering of angels" was given by President Gordon B. Hinckley to the priesthood of the Church, from the Tabernacle on Temple Square, 19 May 1985.

4. Charles W. Penrose, *Masterpieces of Latter-day Saint Leaders* (Salt Lake City: Deseret Book Co., 1953), pp. 66–67.

5. *Deseret Weekly News,* 53:642–43.

6. *The Discourses of Wilford Woodruff* (Salt Lake City: Bookcraft, 1969), pp. 298–300.

7. *History of the Church,* 2:381.

8. Matthias F. Cowley, *Wilford Woodruff* (Salt Lake City: Bookcraft, 1964), p. 130.

9. Harold B. Lee, Conference Report, April 1973, p. 179.

10. Joseph F. Smith, Conference Report, April 1916, pp. 2–3.

11. *Melvin J. Ballard—Crusader for Righteousness,* p. 219.

12. *History of the Church,* 2:381.

13. Harold B. Lee, Conference Report, October 1972, p. 18.

14. Ibid., p. 176.

Chapter 7. Temples: Our Link with Eternity

1. A report by Simon Baker in Journal History, under date of 15 August 1840, LDS Church Archives; cited in *Words of Joseph Smith,* ed. Andrew F. Ehat and Lyndon W. Cook (Provo, Utah: Religious Studies Center, Brigham Young University, 1980), p. 49.

2. See Lucy Mack Smith, *History of Joseph Smith by His Mother,* p. 308; "Nauvoo Baptisms for the Dead," Book A, Church Genealogical Society Archives, pp. 145, 149.

3. *Teachings of the Prophet Joseph Smith,* pp. 179–80; italics added.

4. Ibid., p. 356.

5. Ibid., p. 193.

6. Ibid., p. 158.

7. Ibid., p. 308.

8. See Bruce R. McConkie, *The Millennial Messiah,* pp. 103, 268.

9. Bruce R. McConkie, Conference Report, April 1983, p. 28.

10. *The Millennial Messiah,* p. 264. A more thorough treatment of this subject is Bruce R. McConkie, "The Promises Made to the Fathers," *Studies in Scripture, Vol. 3: The Old Testament, Genesis—2 Samuel,* ed. Kent P. Jackson and Robert L. Millet (Sandy, Utah: Randall Book Co., 1985), pp. 47–62.

11. *Teachings of the Prophet Joseph Smith,* p. 337.

12. Ibid., p. 322.

13. Ibid., p. 338.

14. Why send Elijah? Joseph Smith answered: "Elijah was the last prophet that held the keys of the Priesthood, and who will, before the last dispensation, restore the authority and deliver the keys of the Priesthood, *in order that all the ordinances may be attended to in righteousness."* (*Teachings of the Prophet Joseph Smith,* p. 172; italics added; cf. Joseph Fielding Smith, *Doctrines of Salvation,* 3 vols., comp. Bruce R. McConkie (Salt Lake City: Bookcraft, 1954–56), 2:115–28; Bruce R. McConkie, *Mormon Doctrine,* 2nd ed. (Salt Lake City: Bookcraft, 1966), p. 683.

15. Bruce R. McConkie, *Doctrinal New Testament Commentary,* 1:607.

16. Journal History, 23 February 1847.

17. *Journal of Discourses,* 4:135–36.

18. Ibid., 24:76–77.

19. *Ensign,* January 1977, p. 3.

20. "Bishop John Wells: His Life and Labors," typescript, p. 15, Harold B. Lee Library, Brigham Young University.

21. *Millennial Star,* vol. 58, p. 742.

Chapter 8. When Children Die

1. S. E. Frost, *The Basic Teachings of the Great Philosophers* (New York: The New Home Library, 1942), p. 63.

2. For a discussion of the fact that Adam and Eve's act was *transgression* and not *sin,* see Joseph Fielding Smith, *Doctrines of Salvation,* 1:114. An excellent treatment of the Latter-day Saint view of the Fall is in LaMar Garrard, "The Fall of Man," *Principles of the Gospel in Practice,* Proceedings of the 1985 Sidney B. Sperry Symposium (Sandy, Utah: Randall Book Co., 1985), pp. 39–70.

3. Frost, *Basic Teachings of the Great Philosophers,* pp. 150–51. See also Martin Luther's debate with Erasmus the humanist on the nature of free will in Martin Luther, *The Bondage of the Will,* translated by Henry Cole (Grand Rapids, Michigan: Baker Book House, 1976).

4. This is a particularly interesting heresy. It may well be that the Apostle Paul had reference to this problem in Hebrews 12:24.

5. James E. Talmage, *The Articles of Faith* (Salt Lake City: The Church of Jesus Christ of Latter-day Saints, 1975), p. 126.

6. James E. Talmage, *The Great Apostasy* (Salt Lake City: Deseret Book Co., 1973), p. 119.

7. *Teachings of the Prophet Joseph Smith,* p. 197.

8. Bruce R. McConkie, expressing the sentiments of Joseph Fielding Smith, in "The Salvation of Little Children," *Ensign,* April 1977, p. 6.

9. *Teachings of the Prophet Joseph Smith,* pp. 196–97.

10. From an address at the funeral of Rebecca Adams, 28 October 1967, typescript, pp. 2–3.

11. Bruce R. McConkie, "The Salvation of Little Children," *Ensign,* April 1977, p. 6; see also Joseph Fielding Smith, *Doctrines of Salvation,* 2:55–56.

12. *Doctrines of Salvation,* 2:56–57; italics added; cf. McConkie, "The Salvation of Little Children," *Ensign,* April 1977, p. 6.

13. *Teachings of the Prophet Joseph Smith,* pp. 199–200; italics added.

14. *History of the Church,* 6:316.

15. *Gospel Doctrine,* pp. 452–54; see also an article in the *Improvement Era,* June 1904. For President Smith's discussion of the misunderstanding of Joseph's original teachings, see a sermon entitled "Status of Children in the Resurrection," remarks at a temple fast meeting held in February of 1918, in *Improvement Era,* 21:567–74 (May 1918); cited also in *Messages of the First Presidency,* 6 vols., comp. James R. Clark (Salt Lake City: Bookcraft, 1965–75), 5:91–98.

16. See Joseph Fielding Smith, *Doctrines of Salvation,* 2:54; Bruce R. McConkie, "The Salvation of Little Children," *Ensign,* April 1977, p. 5.

17. *Teachings of the Prophet Joseph Smith,* p. 296.

18. Bruce R. McConkie, "The Salvation of Little Children," *Ensign,* April 1977, p. 7.

Chapter 9. Many Mansions

1. *History of the Church,* 1:245.

Chapter 10. The Gift of Salvation

1. *Lectures on Faith,* 7:9.

2. See *Teachings of the Prophet Joseph Smith,* pp. 297, 301, 305; 1 Corinthians 15:25; Hebrews 2:8.

3. Bruce R. McConkie, *The Promised Messiah* (Salt Lake City: Deseret Book Co., 1978), p. 129; italics added; cf. p. 306; Bruce R. McConkie, *A New Witness for the Articles of Faith* (Salt Lake City: Deseret Book Co., 1985), pp. 144–54.

4. *Teachings of the Prophet Joseph Smith,* pp. 300–301; italics added.

5. See Bruce R. McConkie, *Mormon Doctrine,* p. 238.

6. See *Teachings of the Prophet Joseph Smith,* p. 189; Joseph Fielding Smith, *Doctrines of Salvation,* 1:61.

7. Bruce R. McConkie, "Jesus Christ and Him Crucified," *1976 Brigham Young University Devotional Speeches of the Year* (Provo, Utah: Brigham Young University Press, 1977), pp. 398–401; cf. "The Seven Deadly Heresies," *1980 Brigham Young University Devotional Speeches of the Year* (Provo, Utah: Brigham Young University Press, 1981), pp. 78–79; Conference Report, October 1976, pp. 158–59.

8. *Teachings of the Prophet Joseph Smith,* pp. 149–51.

9. Marion G. Romney, Conference Report, October 1965, p. 20.

10. *Teachings of the Prophet Joseph Smith,* p. 299.

11. From an address at the funeral service for Elder S. Dilworth Young, 13 July 1981, typescript, p. 5; italics added.

Chapter 11. From Everlasting to Everlasting

1. *Journal of Discourses,* 15:249.

2. Boyd K. Packer, Conference Report, October 1983, p. 22.

3. From Joseph F. Smith, John R. Winder, and Anthon H. Lund, "The Origin of Man," *Improvement Era,* 13:75–81 (November 1909); also in *Messages of the First Presidency,* 4:200–206; italics added.

4. Bruce R. McConkie, *The Mortal Messiah,* 1:23.

5. Harold B. Lee, Conference Report, October 1973, pp. 5–8.

6. *Teachings of the Prophet Joseph Smith,* p. 343.

7. Ibid.

8. Ibid., pp. 345–46.

9. *Journal of Discourses,* 11:249.

10. Ibid., 13:57.

11. *Lectures on Faith,* 4:11.

12. Ibid., 4:5–19.

13. Bruce R. McConkie, "The Lord God of Joseph Smith," *Brigham Young University Devotional Addresses* (Provo, Utah: Brigham Young University Press, 1972), January 1972, p. 7. Elder McConkie is here making reference to a statement from the *Times and Seasons,* 5:758.

14. *Teachings of the Prophet Joseph Smith,* pp. 347–48; italics added.

15. *Lectures on Faith,* 5:2.

16. From Eliza R. Snow Smith, *Biography and Family Record of Lorenzo Snow* (Salt Lake City: Deseret News Co., Printers, 1884), pp. 9–10.

17. Ibid., pp. 46–47.

18. *Improvement Era,* 22:660–61 (June 1919).

19. *Teachings of the Prophet Joseph Smith,* pp. 346–47.

Chapter 12. That All May Be Saved

1. Hugh Nibley, *When the Lights Went Out* (Salt Lake City: Deseret Book Co., 1976), pp. 35–36.

2. J. A. MacCulloch, *The Harrowing of Hell* (Edinburgh: T. & T. Clark, 1930), p. 31.

3. Ibid., p. 32.

4. Ibid.

5. 2 Maccabees 12:45.

6. Louis Ginzberg, *The Legends of the Jews,* 7 vols. (Philadelphia: The Jewish Publication Society of America, 1968), 6:332.

7. Ibid., 3:97.

8. *The Harrowing of Hell,* pp. 48–49.

9. Ibid., p. 84–85.

10. Ibid., p. 104.

11. Alexander Roberts and James Donaldson, ed., *Ante-Nicene Fathers,* 10 vols. (Grand Rapids: Wm. B. Eerdmans Publishing Co., 1981), 1:494.

12. Ibid., 2:490–91.

13. Ibid., p. 491.

14. Ibid.

15. Ibid., p. 492.

16. *The Harrowing of Hell,* pp. 244–47.

17. James H. Charlesworth, ed., *The Old Testament Pseudepigrapha,* 2 vols. (New York: Doubleday & Company, Inc., 1985), 2:750–51.

18. Ibid., pp. 754, 757, 771.

19. *The Harrowing of Hell,* p. 135.

Glossary

Abraham's Bosom. This is a term used by Christ to describe the paradise of God (Luke 16:22). Since Abraham was known as the father of the faithful, this phrase carries with it the idea that in death the righteous will enjoy the company of their faithful fathers. Joseph of Egypt expressed the principle thus, "I die," he said, "and go unto my fathers; and I go down to my grave with joy" (JST Genesis 50:24).

Angels. Literally, angels are messengers. Angels are the spirit offspring of God. An angel of the Lord is one who bears a divine message. In the scriptures the following are referred to as angels: (1) the pre-earth Christ, usually under the title "the angel of the Lord," or the "angel of his presence" (Genesis 22:11–12; Abraham 1:15; D&C 133:53); (2) pre-earth spirits: for instance, the angel who appeared to Adam and asked why he was offering sacrifices (Moses 5:6–8), for no angels minister to this earth except those who belong to it (D&C 130:5); (3) translated beings, such as the Three Nephites (3 Nephi 28:30) and John the Revelator (D&C 7:6); (4) spirits of just men made perfect, the righteous now in paradise. Because of their obedience to gospel law, they have the sure promise that in the resurrection they will be made perfect (D&C 129:3). Such men as Joseph Smith, Brigham Young, and John Taylor would be examples (D&C 138:53); (5) resurrected beings, those angels with bodies of flesh and bone (D&C 129:1–2) like John the Baptist and Moroni; (6) righteous mortal men, those mortal men who are occasionally referred to as angels in the scriptures (JST Genesis 19:15).

Satan and the one-third of the host of heaven who were cast out for rebelling against Christ and God are also referred to as angels (Revelation 12:9).

Buffetings of Satan. To be delivered over to the buffetings of Satan is to be given unto the devil. "It is to be turned over to him with all the protective power of the priesthood, of righteousness, and of godliness removed, so that Lucifer is free to torment, persecute, and afflict such a person without let or hindrance. When the bars are down, the cuffs and curses of Satan, both in this world and in the world to come, bring indescribable anguish typified by burning fire and brimstone. The damned in hell so suffer." (Bruce R. McConkie, *Mormon Doctrine,* p. 108; see D&C 78:12; 82:20–21; 104:9–10; 1 Corinthians 5:1–5.)

Church of the Firstborn. The Church of the Firstborn is the church of the exalted, an organization beyond the veil whose membership consists of those who have overcome the world and are thus qualified for exaltation in the celestial kingdom. It is that "inner circle" of individuals who, as the elect of God, have become joint heirs with Christ to all the Father has, and are thus in a position to inherit equally with the Only Begotten. In short, these are entitled to the blessings of the Firstborn. (D&C 76:54, 67, 94; 88:5; 93:22.)

Eternal Life. "Eternal" is one of the names of God, and thus to possess eternal life is to enjoy God's life. More specifically, eternal life consists of: (1) the continuation of the family unit in eternity; and (2) inheriting, receiving, and possessing the fulness of the glory of the Father. (D&C 132:19.)

Eternal Lives. To have eternal lives is "to know the only wise and true God, and Jesus Christ, whom he hath sent" (D&C 132:24; cf. John 17:3). To have eternal lives is to have eternal life, or exaltation. The phrase *eternal lives* lays stress upon the right of a worthy husband and wife to have posterity in the worlds to come.

Exaltation. To have exaltation is to possess eternal life, to be entitled to the blessings of the highest degree of the celestial kingdom. The word *exaltation* lays stress upon the elevated and ennobled status of one who so qualifies for the society of the redeemed and glorified.

Heir. An heir is one entitled to a family inheritance. Jesus Christ is the rightful heir to all that the Father has (Romans 4:13–14; Hebrews 1:1–4). Those who receive the new and everlasting covenant, partake of the ordinances of salvation, enjoy the gifts of the spirit and blessings of Church membership, and endure faithfully to the end will eventually become join heirs—coinheritors—with Jesus Christ to the fulness of the Father (Romans 8:14–18).

Hell. An English translation of the Hebrew word *Sheol,* hell signifies an abode of departed spirits and corresponds to the Greek *Hades.* It originally carried this broad meaning with both Jew and Christian. For instance, the King James translators interpreted Peter as saying that Christ at his death went to hell (Acts 2:27). Joseph Smith in his translation changed the verse to read *prison.* In either case the meaning is the same—Christ went to the world of spirits. We know, however, that he did not go among the wicked (D&C 138:20–22, 29–30). Hades or hell was believed to consist of two parts, *paradise and Gehenna,* the former being the abode of the righteous and the latter the abode of the disobedient. In common speech, hell has come to mean the place of torment for the wicked and is also so used in many scriptural texts (2 Nephi 28:22).

Among the Apostolic Fathers, Gehenna came to be thought of as a place of everlasting torment, while Hades was spoken of as a place of purgation. The just, according to their thought, were consigned to Hades to await the Savior who would eventually free them from this state so that they might go to heaven. The vicious sinners, however, remained in Gehenna, from which predicament they could not be freed.

Immortal. The resurrected body is said to be "spiritual and immortal," in the sense that it shall live forever, is not subject to death, and will never again know corruption (Alma 11:45).

Judgment. Many partial judgements will precede the great day of judgment. Death is a judgment in that the spirit will receive an inheritance either in paradise or hell. The resurrection is a judgment: those coming forth in the morning of the first resurrection are assured of their place in the celestial kingdom; those in the afternoon of the first resurrection are assured of their place in the terrestrial kingdom, and so on. It is only after the resurrection that we "appear before the judgment seat of the Holy One of Israel" to be judged according to our works (2 Nephi 9:15–16). In a very real sense, each day of our lives is also a judgment, for we are daily writing the book of life out of which we will be judged (Revelation 20:11–15).

Justification. It is a requirement of heaven that anything that is to be of "efficacy, virtue, or force in and after the resurrection from the dead" must be entered into and performed in righteousness. Only those who have lived their covenants with exactness and honor can be justified by the Holy Spirit of Promise (the Holy Ghost), who must ratify or approve their worthiness for the blessings promised in the ordinance and covenants they have made. (D&C 132:5–7.)

Keys. Keys are directing powers, the right of presidency, and the one having them holds the reins of government. The presiding officer in the various quorums and auxiliaries of the Church holds the keys or the rights and responsibilities of presidency.

Outer Darkness. The portion of the spirit world known as hell is also identified in scripture as "outer darkness" (Alma 40:13–14; D&C 138:22, 30, 57). "So complete is the darkness prevailing in the minds of these spirits, so wholly has gospel light been shut out of the consciences, that they know little or nothing of the plan of salvation, and have little hope within themselves of advancement and progression through the saving grace of Christ" (Bruce R. McConkie, *Mormon Doctrine,* pp. 551–52).

Paradise. Paradise is a Persian word meaning "a garden." It is used in the Book of Mormon to describe the abode of righteous spirits between death and the resurrection (Alma 40:12, 14). The term is not used in the Old Testament, and is used only three times in the New Testament (Luke 23:43; 2 Corinthians 12:4; Revelation 2:7). Its

New Testament usage is vague. Joseph Smith tells us that the words attributed to Christ and directed to the thief on the cross should read: "This day shalt thou be with me in the world of spirits" (*Teaching of the Prophet Joseph Smith,* p. 309). *Paradise* is used only twice in Doctrine and Covenants, where it is a synonym for heaven (D&C 77:2, 5). The Book of Mormon usage has prevailed in Latter-day Saint theology. Adam's paradisiacal state is a symbolic representation of the temple (Joseph Fielding McConkie, *Gospel Symbolism,* p. 258), and thus paradise would naturally become in death the abode of those who are worthy to enter the temple.

Presence of God. To return to "the presence of God" at death is to go into the world of spirits, a realm wherein the Spirit of God, or Light of Christ—that spiritual influence which is in and through all things and the means whereby God is omnipresent—may be felt. To be "taken home to that God who gave [us] life" (Alma 40:11; cf. Ecclesiastes 12:7) thus has no reference to going directly into the immediate presence of our God.

Rest of the Lord. To enter into the rest of the Lord is: (1) to enjoy the spiritual peace and assurance that comes from a settled conviction as to the truthfulness of the latter-day work, an unshaken witness of the Lord and the work of his anointed servants (Joseph F. Smith, *Gospel Doctrine,* pp. 58, 126); (2) by extension, to qualify for entrance into paradise at the time of death. Moses sought to bring the children of Israel into the rest of the Lord, to bring them through the veil into the presence of God, that they might receive the fulness of his glory (D&C 84:24).

Resurrection. A resurrected being is one for whom body and spirit are inseparably connected, never again to know death, disease, or corruption of any kind (Alma 11:45; D&C 138:17).

Salvation. Salvation is the greatest of all the gifts of God (D&C 6:13; 14:7). To be saved is to have eternal life and thus to be qualified to receive exaltation in the celestial kingdom. The word *salvation* lays stress upon one's saved condition, his state being one of deliverance from death and sin through the atoning sacrifice of Jesus Christ.

Spirit Prison. A synonym for "spirit world," it includes the abode of both the righteous and the wicked. For instance, the faithful Saints of dispensations past while in the spirit world were spoken of as "captives" seeking "liberty" because they were in the "chains of death" (D&C 138:18). Paradise is a part of spirit prison because the dead look "upon the long absence of their spirits from their bodies as a bondage" (D&C 138:50).

Spiritual. Bodies are said to be "spiritual" in the sense that they are immortal and thus not subject to death (Alma 11:45; D&C 88:27; Moses 3:9; 1 Corinthians 15:44).

Index

About the Authors

Robert L. Millet, professor of ancient scripture and former dean of Religious Education at Brigham Young University, taught in the Church Educational System before joining the faculty at BYU in 1983. He earned a master's degree in psychology from BYU and a Ph.D. in religious studies from Florida State University.

He has served in The Church of Jesus Christ of Latter-day Saints as a bishop, stake president, temple worker, and member of the Church Materials Evaluation Committee. He is a prolific speaker and writer. His recent books include *Grace Works, Lost and Found: Reflections on the Prodigal Son,* and *More Holiness Give Me.*

Brother Millet and his wife, Shauna Sizemore Millet, are the parents of six children.

Joseph Fielding McConkie is a professor of ancient scripture at Brigham Young University. Before joining the faculty at BYU, he taught seminary and served as director of the institute of religion at the University of Washington in Seattle. He also presided over the Scotland Edinburgh Mission of The Church of Jesus Christ of Latter-day Saints. A prolific writer, he is the author or coauthor of numerous works, including *Here We Stand, Gospel Symbolism, Sons and Daughters of God,* and the four-volume *Doctrinal Commentary on the Book of Mormon.* He and his wife, Brenda Kempton McConkie, are the parents of nine children. The family resides in Orem, Utah.